Brand New From Ripley's!

The astounding team from Ripley's has done it again—and what a job they've done. Strange, startling, weird, and wonderful, these oddest of oddities from the remotest corners of the globe are as fascinating as they are fantastic—and, of course, every single one is true!

If you cannot find your favorite **Believe It or Not!** POCKET BOOK at your local newsstand, please write to the nearest Ripley's "Believe It or Not!" museum:

19 San Marco Avenue,
St. Augustine, Florida 32084

901 North Ocean Blvd.,
Myrtle Beach, South Carolina 29577

175 Jefferson Street,
San Francisco, California 94133

145 East Elkhorn Avenue,
Estes Park, Colorado 80517

Rebel Corners,
Gatlinburg, Tennessee 37738

1500 North Wells Street,
Chicago, Illinois 60610

4960 Clifton Hill,
Niagara Falls, Canada L2G 3N5

Boardwalk and Wicomico,
Ocean City, Maryland 21842

Ripley's Believe It or Not! titles

Published by POCKET BOOKS

Ripley's
Believe It or Not!®

29th SERIES

PUBLISHED BY POCKET BOOKS NEW YORK

Another *Original* publication of POCKET BOOKS

POCKET BOOKS, a Simon & Schuster division of
GULF & WESTERN CORPORATION
1230 Avenue of the Americas, New York, N.Y. 10020

Copyright © 1978 by Ripley International Limited

Published by arrangement with Ripley International Limited

ISBN: 0-671-82065-6

First Pocket Books printing November, 1978

1   2   9   8

Trademarks registered in the United States and other countries.

Printed in the U.S.A.

PREFACE

While the number 29 may not have the flash and dazzle of some more showy numbers (The "Twenty-Nine" Commandments? Tea for twenty-nine?), still it must have its points—countless women all over the world elect to remain twenty-nine for years.

Now this discreet, self-effacing figure has something new to celebrate—the book you have in hand is twenty-ninth in the *Ripley's Believe It or Not!* series. And in keeping with our custom, we'd like to pay a little homage now to the number of our latest edition.

It was October 29, 1929, that the stock market crashed, the Dow Jones plunging 122 points!

It was November 29, 1926, that the United States Supreme Court upheld the "Dry Law" prohibiting whiskey consumption except with a doctor's prescription.

In was in 29 A.D. that Jesus Christ was crucified, according to calculations by Dr. Oswald Gerhard of Berlin.

And November 29, 1886, was the day travelers in Scranton, Pennsylvania, climbed aboard the first electric streetcar to collect fares!

Lest 29 came to connote calamity and bother, we might add that 1829 marked the arrival of the original Siamese twins in Boston on August 16. Chang and Eng, joined together at the waist, struggled for 63 years to live their separate lives. Both married and fathered a total of 22 children.

And, of course, it was in 1829 that the first reference to baked beans appeared in a book entitled *The Frugal Housewife*. Finally, it was in 1929 that the Ripley's Believe It or Not! feature was syndicated worldwide!

With that, we bid you welcome to our 29th collection of fascinating people, places, and things, all of them fun to read about, and all of them *absolutely true*—Believe It or Not!

Ripley International Ltd.
Toronto, Canada

Ripley's Believe It or Not!

THE HIGHEST GOLF COURSE IN THE WORLD
Cerro de Pasco, Peru,
14,300 FEET ABOVE SEA LEVEL

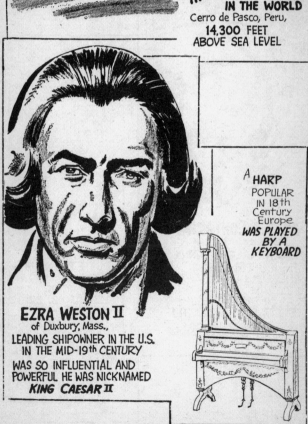

A **HARP**
POPULAR IN 18th Century Europe
WAS PLAYED BY A KEYBOARD

EZRA WESTON II
of Duxbury, Mass.,
LEADING SHIPOWNER IN THE U.S. IN THE MID-19th CENTURY
WAS SO INFLUENTIAL AND POWERFUL HE WAS NICKNAMED
KING CAESAR II

9

NATURAL CRUCIFIX

Church of Maria Strasengel, Austria — A PLANT THAT GREW IN THE SHAPE OF A CRUCIFIX

ANDREA CONTARINI
(1296-1382)

ELECTED DOGE OF VENICE, THE HIGHEST POST IN THE REPUBLIC, **3** TIMES REFUSED TO ACCEPT THE HONOR —UNTIL HE WAS ORDERED TO ASSUME IT **UNDER PAIN OF DEATH!**

HE SERVED AS DOGE FOR 14 YEARS

A *PARROT* SAVED THE LIFE OF LEO, SON OF EMPEROR BASIL OF THE BYZANTINE EMPIRE, WHO WAS ABOUT TO BE EXECUTED BY HIS FATHER, BECAUSE THE PARROT HAD BEEN TRAINED TO CRY **"POOR LEO"**

EMPEROR BASIL SPARED HIS SON AND LEO BECAME RULER OF HALF THE ROMAN WORLD 880

THE REV. ARTHUR WAGNER (1850-1902) of Brighton, England,

CONSTRUCTED 5 CHURCHES IN THAT COMMUNITY AT HIS OWN EXPENSE - SPENDING HIS ENTIRE FORTUNE OF MORE THAN $375,000

ANTONIO BIENVENIDA famed Spanish bullfighter

IS THE SON AND GRANDSON OF MATADORS, NEPHEW OF 3 MATADORS, AND BROTHER OF 2 MATADORS

RAMPSIDE HALL near Barrow-in-Furness, England, *WAS BUILT WITH 12 CHIMNEYS* —

SO EACH OF THE OWNER'S 12 SONS COULD HAVE A ROOM WITH A FIREPLACE 1608

NUTTALL'S POORWILLS COUSINS OF THE WHIPPOORWILL **HIBERNATE**

THE **AARDVARK** SPENDS THE DAY UNDERGROUND IN TUNNELS, *EMERGING ONLY AT NIGHT*

FRANÇOIS EPERVIER of Paris, France, WAS SO CERTAIN THE RULE OF EMPEROR NAPOLEON III WOULD BE BRIEF THAT HE VOWED HE WOULD DRINK A GLASS OF WATER *EVERY HOUR OF NAPOLEON'S REIGN* HE ACTUALLY DRANK A GLASS OF WATER EVERY WAKING HOUR *FOR 18 YEARS !*

THE **YOUNGEST FATHER**

Richard Michael FATHER

WAS BORN ON FATHER'S DAY Albany, N.Y.

12

THE DESSERT
SERVED BY KING
JAMES V of Scotland
TO EACH GUEST
AT A BANQUET
*CONSISTED OF A
DEEP DISH FILLED
WITH GOLD PIECES*

MRS MARTHA WALDO LINCOLN
THE MOTHER OF 2
NEW ENGLAND GOVERNORS,
GAVE 3 SUCCESSIVE SONS
THE FIRST NAME OF WALDO
*-AND SAW ALL 3
DIE IN INFANCY*
SHE THEN GAVE HER
NEXT TWO BOYS WALDO
AS THEIR MIDDLE
NAME —AND BOTH
SURVIVED TO MANHOOD

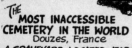

THE MOST INACCESSIBLE CEMETERY IN THE WORLD
Douzes, France
*A GRAVEYARD LOCATED ATOP THE
GREAT ROCK OF SAINT-GERVALS
700 FEET ABOVE THE JONTE RIVER*

MANY POST OFFICES
in East Bengal,
Pakistan,
TO BETTER SERVE
THE POPULACE
*ARE LOCATED
ON BOATS*

LINCOLN DRUGS
in Oak Park, Mich.,
HAS A TELEPHONE NUMBER
THAT SPELLS OUT ITS NAME
LI 3-7847
(D RUGS)

T^{HE}**FIRST ORANGE TREE IN ITALY**
PLANTED IN THE GARDENS OF
SANTA SABINA, ROME, IN 1216
IS STILL GROWING 746 YEARS LATER

"*NOOWOMANTAMOOONKAUUNONNASH*"

SAY IT
AGAIN!

IN THE LANGUAGE OF THE
ALGONQUIN INDIANS
MEANS "LOVE"

14

LADIES in Purang, Tibet, USE ONLY ONE COSMETIC — *SOOT!*

THE MEETING HOUSE GRAVEYARD in Old Sturbridge Village, Mass., IS FULL OF AUTHENTIC TOMBSTONES — *YET IT DOESN'T HAVE A SINGLE GRAVE.*

THE REVOLVING ROCK
Trancoso, Portugal,
A **BOULDER** WEIGHING **30** TONS, SO DELICATELY BALANCED ON ITS NATURAL STONE PIVOT THAT THE *ROTATION OF THE EARTH SPINS IT HALFWAY AROUND EACH DAY!*

CHRISTIAN SCHMALZ
of West Hempstead, N.Y.,
HAD
- 8 *CHILDREN*
- 8 *GRANDCHILDREN*
- 8 *GREAT-GRANDCHILDREN*

THE REV. THOMAS COLE
MINISTER OF LIZARD POINT, England,

WALKED **26** MILES IN ONE DAY TO VISIT A SICK PARISHIONER *WHEN HE WAS* **120** *YEARS OF AGE*

AN **OFFICIAL PROCLAMATION** SEALED WITH WAX IS POSTED OVER CROPS in Purnea, India, **TO FRIGHTEN AWAY INSECTS**

HORN-SHAPED SEA SHELLS ARE USED BY CHILDREN in India *AS SPINNING TOPS*

BEER IS BREWED BY the Nyoro Tribe of Bunyoro, Africa, BY MIXING COOKED BANANAS WITH SWEET GRASS AND WATER *AND STAMPING ON IT FOR HOURS WITH BARE FEET*

MEXICAN BEAN MARKED BY NATURE WITH A PERFECT **5**

Submitted by MRS. LYDIA DAVILA, Los Angeles, Calif.

17

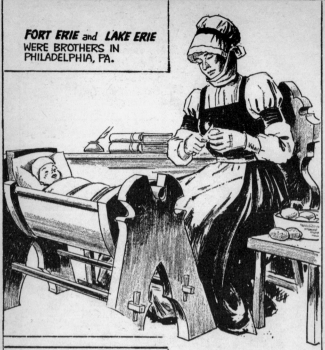

FORT ERIE and **LAKE ERIE** WERE BROTHERS IN PHILADELPHIA, PA.

THE LIVING GATE

ENTRANCE ARCH TO A TEMPLE in Osaka, Japan, *FORMED BY 2 TALL TREES*

PHEBE RIPLEY (1742-1825) of Concord, Mass., WHO DIDN'T BELIEVE IN WASTING TIME, TAUGHT LATIN AND GREEK TO A CLASS OF HARVARD STUDENTS *WHILE PEELING POTATOES WITH HER HANDS AND ROCKING A CRADLE WITH HER FEET*

AN OAK TREE

STANDING IN EASTON LODGE PARK, near Dunmow, England, FOR 1,000 YEARS, WAS DYING IN 1944 UNTIL A WORLD WAR II BOMB DUMP EXPLODED NEARBY— *IT HAS FLOURISHED EVER SINCE*

THE REV. JOSEF BÖCK (1804-1900) WAS A PASTOR IN Guntramsdorf, Austria, FOR 74 YEARS

THE MOST AMAZING POLITICIAN IN ALL HISTORY FENG YAO (881-954) Prime Minister of China, RETAINED HIS POST **THROUGH 9 REVOLUTIONS!** *HE SERVED UNDER 10 EMPERORS AND 5 DIFFERENT DYNASTIES*

COINS

ONCE WERE MADE IN the Chad Territory, Africa, **FROM BROKEN PIECES OF POTTERY** *THE MORE JAGGED EDGES THEY HAD THE GREATER THEIR VALUE*

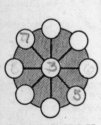

CAN YOU DISTRIBUTE THE DIGITS FROM 1 TO 9 IN THE SMALL CIRCLES *SO THAT EACH LINE ADDS UP TO 15 ?*

John, **EARL of WORCESTER** 1427 - 1470 SENTENCED TO DEATH IN LONDON, England, AS ATONEMENT FOR HIS MANY ACTS OF CRUELTY *ORDERED THE HEADSMAN TO TAKE 3 STROKES*

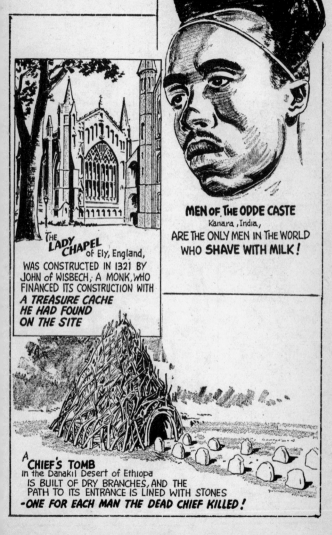

THE **LADY CHAPEL** of Ely, England, WAS CONSTRUCTED IN 1321 BY JOHN of WISBECH, A MONK, WHO FINANCED ITS CONSTRUCTION WITH *A TREASURE CACHE HE HAD FOUND ON THE SITE*

MEN OF THE ODDE CASTE
Kanara, India,
ARE THE ONLY MEN IN THE WORLD
WHO **SHAVE WITH MILK!**

A **CHIEF'S TOMB** in the Danakil Desert of Ethiopa IS BUILT OF DRY BRANCHES, AND THE PATH TO ITS ENTRANCE IS LINED WITH STONES - *ONE FOR EACH MAN THE DEAD CHIEF KILLED!*

MEMBERS of the Rodiya Tribe, in Ceylon, **BECAUSE AN ANCESTRESS NAMED PRINCESS VALLI BECAME A CANNIBAL, HAVE BEEN OUTCASTS FOR 800 YEARS** *EVERY RODIYA WOMAN MUST USE THE NAME VALLI AND EACH MAN IS CALLED VILLIYA —AND NONE MAY EAT MORE THAN A SINGLE MEAL A DAY*

THE DEATH OF A COW in Liechtenstein IS ALWAYS ANNOUNCED *BY AN OBITUARY IN THE LOCAL NEWSPAPER*

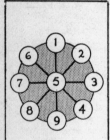

(Answer) HOW TO DISTRIBUTE THE DIGITS FROM 1 TO 9 IN THE SMALL CIRCLES SO THAT EACH LINE ADDS UP TO 15

ALEXANDER COCHRANE of Dundonald, Scotland, WAS THE FATHER OF 7 COLONELS *ALL OF WHOM SERVED IN THE ARMY OF KING CHARLES I*

THE 10-DALER COPPER COIN of Sweden WORTH $7.20 WAS 27½ INCHES LONG, NEARLY A FOOT WIDE, AND WEIGHED 44 POUNDS

THE IRON PAGODA OF HONAN, China, BUILT 800 YEARS AGO IN THE BELIEF ITS WEIGHT WOULD HOLD DOWN THE GROUND --

AND SO PREVENT EARTHQUAKES!

ALEXANDER ADAM (1741-1809)
A HIGH SCHOOL TEACHER IN EDINBURGH, SCOTLAND, FOR 48 YEARS, COULD RECALL THE BIRTH DATE, MARKS AND OTHER PERTINENT FACTS ABOUT *EVERY STUDENT HE EVER TAUGHT*

CH'ING
Chief of the Chinese Beggars' Guild

RULED ALL CHINA AND ITS 400,000,000 PEOPLE FOR 3 YEARS!

FROM 1908 TO 1911 CH'ING ASSIGNED STREET CORNERS TO BEGGARS AND AT THE SAME TIME SERVED AS REGENT FOR HSUAN T'UNG-- WHO BECAME EMPEROR AT THE AGE OF 2½

SICKLES WERE ORIGINALLY MADE BY THE ANCIENT EGYPTIANS FROM *THE JAWBONES OF OXEN*

A WOODEN BAR
LINKING 2 TREES
IN ZION, Va.,
HAS REMAINED
IN PLACE
SINCE 1790
- WHEN IT
SERVED AS AN
IMPROVISED
PULPIT
FOR THE
COMMUNITY'S
FIRST
SERVICES

Dorothea Lynde DIX
1802 - 1889
OPENED A SCHOOL IN
WORCESTER, MASS., FOR THE
CHILDREN OF ITS ARISTOCRACY
*WHEN SHE HERSELF WAS
ONLY 14 YEARS OF AGE*

THE **GATE** TO A FARM IN
Boughton Monchelsea, England,
IS TOPPED BY A STONE SHAPED
LIKE A ROUND LOAF OF BREAD
- *A WARNING TO MEDIEVAL
BAKERS AGAINST CHEATING
IN THE WEIGHT OF THEIR LOAVES*

A MOHAMMEDAN MOSQUE

WITH A MINARET 225 FEET HIGH WAS CONSTRUCTED in Lednice, Czechoslovakia

-WHICH HAS NEVER HAD A MOHAMMEDAN RESIDENT-

PRINCE ALOIS LICHTENSTEIN ORDERED THE MOSQUE BUILT AT A COST OF $400,000 IN 1797

TO PUNISH THE TOWN FOR ITS FAILURE TO PROVIDE HIM WITH A SUITABLE SITE FOR A CHURCH

THE CAPYBARA IS THE LARGEST RODENT *IT WEIGHS 100 LB.*

THE RAINSPOUT ON A HOUSE on the island of Helgoland, Germany, *WAS AN OLD LEATHER BOOT*

A CROCODILE WHEN NEWLY HATCHED *IS 3 TIMES AS LARGE AS THE EGG FROM WHICH IT EMERGED*

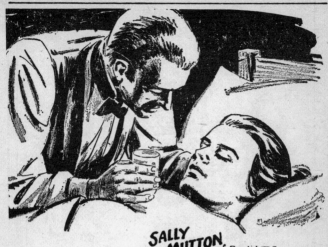

SALLY MUTTON of Bristol, R.I., WAS PRONOUNCED DEAD IN 1900, BUT HER HUSBAND REFUSED TO ACCEPT THE DOCTOR'S STATEMENT -AND HELD OFF THE UNDERTAKER WITH A SHOTGUN

HE POURED HOT MILK BETWEEN HIS WIFE'S LIPS -AND SHE REGAINED CONSCIOUSNESS AND SURVIVED *HER HUSBAND BY 40 YEARS*

The "ʰ" TREE
Submitted by
M.M. MIXSON,
Micanopy, Fla.

IN 8 HORSE RACES at Santa Anita Park, Arcadia, Calif., ALL RUN ON THE SAME DAY *EACH WAS WON BY A HORSE IN A DIFFERENT POST POSITION* (Feb. 6, 1963)

CHINESE BOXERS

FIGHT MATCHES IN WHICH THEY STRIKE BLOWS ONLY *WITH THEIR KNEES*

THE FIRST MAN TO LOSE HIS BALANCE FORFEITS THE CONTEST

THE DEVIL'S CHAIR
NATURAL FORMATION OF VOLCANIC GRANITE NEAR PUERTO NATALES, CHILE
Submitted by RICHARD FINNEY
Coral Gables, Fla.

AND I WAS GOING SWIMMING!

Worcester, N.Y.,
HAD 2 HEAVY SNOWFALLS ON JULY 18, 1876

28

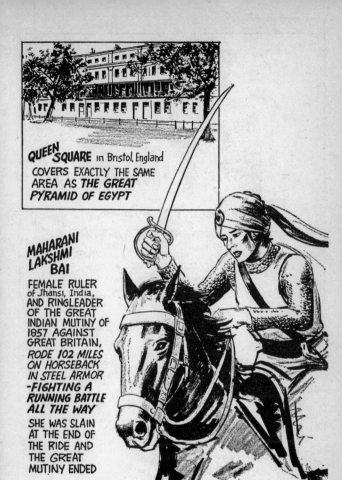

QUEEN SQUARE in Bristol, England COVERS EXACTLY THE SAME AREA AS *THE GREAT PYRAMID OF EGYPT*

MAHARANI LAKSHMI BAI
FEMALE RULER of Jhansi, India, AND RINGLEADER OF THE GREAT INDIAN MUTINY OF 1857 AGAINST GREAT BRITAIN, *RODE 102 MILES ON HORSEBACK IN STEEL ARMOR -FIGHTING A RUNNING BATTLE ALL THE WAY* SHE WAS SLAIN AT THE END OF THE RIDE AND THE GREAT MUTINY ENDED

THE FIRST **20** MOVES IN CHESS CAN HAVE **169,518,829,100,544,000,000,000,000** VARIATIONS

THE MOSQUE of GHARDAIA
in Algeria
SERVES AS A LOST-AND-FOUND DEPARTMENT
VALUABLES FOUND IN THE COMMUNITY
ARE PLACED ON DISPLAY IN ITS WINDOWS
UNTIL THEY ARE CLAIMED BY
THEIR RIGHTFUL OWNERS

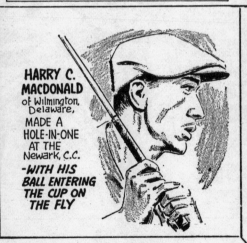

HARRY C. MACDONALD
of Wilmington, Delaware,

MADE A HOLE-IN-ONE AT THE Newark, C.C.

-WITH HIS BALL ENTERING THE CUP ON THE FLY

Lawrence R. Dwight of Fortuna, Calif.,
CELEBRATED HIS FIRST BIRTHDAY
IN THE COMPANY OF 7
OF HIS GREAT-GRANDPARENTS

A HUGE BOULDER SHAPED LIKE AN EGG AND WEIGHING 1,000 POUNDS WAS MOVED FROM YONKERS, N.Y., TO RIDGEFIELD, CONN., BY PAUL CORBALIS -AN INHERITANCE THAT HAS BEEN *PASSED DOWN IN HIS FAMILY FOR 5 GENERATIONS*

THE FALTER TOWER Kitzingen, Germany, **LEANS NEARLY 3 FEET FROM THE PERPENDICULAR**

THE GREAT PAN ROAD up the Sacred Mountain of Tai Shan, China, HAS A SERIES OF HAIRPIN CURVES *-SO EVIL SPIRITS WILL HURTLE OVER THE PRECIPICES*

KEITH M. HENRY
of Knoxville, Tenn.,
RODE
THE SAME MOTORCYCLE
FOR 50 YEARS

GRANDFATHER
*NATURAL
STONE PROFILE*
Grandfather Mountain, N.C.

THE **CHILEAN BEAVER**
IS THE ONLY MAMMAL IN NATURE THAT
FEEDS ITS OFFSPRING ON ITS BACK

Thomas TELFORD

(1757-1834) FAMED SCOTTISH ENGINEER, CONSTRUCTED 920 MILES OF ROADS AND **1,200 BRIDGES**

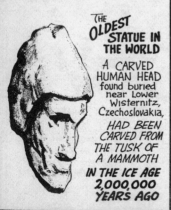

THE OLDEST STATUE IN THE WORLD

A CARVED HUMAN HEAD found buried near Lower Wisternitz, Czechoslovakia, HAD BEEN CARVED FROM THE TUSK OF A MAMMOTH IN THE ICE AGE 2,000,000 YEARS AGO

THE PUBLIC CLOCK in the Borghese Park, Rome, Italy, IS RUN SOLELY ON **WATER POWER**

A **MACKEREL**
PLACED IN A SMALL TANK
OF WATER **WILL DROWN**
*IT IS FORCED TO SWIM
SLOWLY AND ITS
GILLS CANNOT
SUPPLY ENOUGH
OXYGEN TO KEEP
THE FISH ALIVE*

A **BRIDE** in the Chaamba Tribe
of Southern Algeria
IS OFFICIALLY MARRIED
ONLY AFTER HER
HUSBAND HAS
SLAPPED HER 7 TIMES
*SHE MUST THANK HIM
FOR HIS ATTENTION AND
THIS IS THE FIRST AND
LAST TIME IN HER
LIFETIME SHE MAY CALL
HER HUSBAND BY NAME*

THE REV. CHARLES FRASER
of Elland, England,
WHILE A NAVAL CHAPLAIN
IN THE 19th CENTURY
PREACHED IN 7 COUNTRIES
*–ALWAYS IN THE
LANGUAGE OF THE AREA*
HE DELIVERED HIS SERMONS IN
ENGLISH, GREEK, HEBREW, LATIN,
ITALIAN, FRENCH AND SPANISH

SIR EDWARD CARSON WAS THE ONLY MAN IN HISTORY TO HOLD THE POST OF SOLICITOR GENERAL *IN BOTH ENGLAND AND IRELAND*

TALL PAGODA IN Tokyo, Japan, ORIGINALLY STOOD IN Seoul, Korea, THE JAPANESE EMPEROR'S WEDDING GIFT TO THE EMPEROR OF KOREA BUT IN 1910 THE JAPANESE TOOK IT BACK

The **MASHCOS**
of Peru
FAMED AS
WARRIORS
*LONG WORE THEIR
MILITARY RANK
ON THEIR FACES*

EACH TIME A MAN
ADVANCED IN RANK
ANOTHER LEAF WAS
THRUST INTO HIS SKIN

The **BELL** ATOP
KORBACH HIGH SCHOOL,
in Germany,
INSTALLED THE DAY
ON WHICH
PROFESSORS KOENIG,
WALDSCHMIDT AND
WALDECK JOINED THE
SCHOOL, CRACKED AND
BECAME UNUSABLE
50 YEARS LATER
*ON THE DAY THE 3
TEACHERS RETIRED*
April 1, 1901

Dogs
RIDING IN MOTOR CARS
IN THE EARLY DAYS OF
THE AUTOMOBILE
*OFTEN WORE GOGGLES
AND SPECIAL ATTIRE*

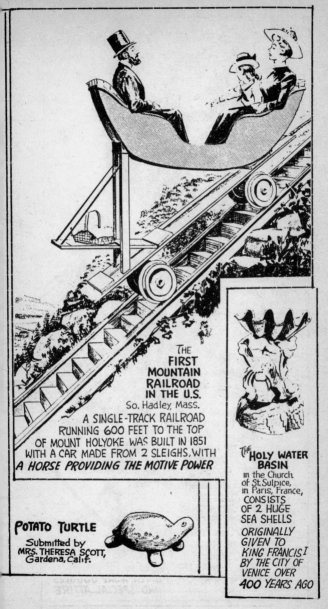

THE FIRST MOUNTAIN RAILROAD IN THE U.S.
So. Hadley, Mass.

A SINGLE-TRACK RAILROAD RUNNING 600 FEET TO THE TOP OF MOUNT HOLYOKE WAS BUILT IN 1851 WITH A CAR MADE FROM 2 SLEIGHS, WITH *A HORSE PROVIDING THE MOTIVE POWER*

THE HOLY WATER BASIN
in the Church of St. Sulpice, in Paris, France, CONSISTS OF 2 HUGE SEA SHELLS

ORIGINALLY GIVEN TO KING FRANCIS I BY THE CITY OF VENICE OVER **400** *YEARS AGO*

POTATO TURTLE
Submitted by MRS. THERESA SCOTT, Gardena, Calif.

THE REV. HENRY DIXON
of Big Sandy Valley, Ky.,
AN ACCOMPLISHED VIOLINIST,
ALWAYS PLAYED THE FIDDLE
TO ENTERTAIN PARISHIONERS
*BEFORE AND AFTER
EACH SERVICE*

**CAPTAIN
THOMAS
WEST
PEYTON IV**
of
Huntington, W.Va.,
WHO FOUGHT IN
WORLD WAR I
*WAS THE SON
OF CAPT. THOMAS
WEST PEYTON III*
OF THE **CIVIL WAR**
*THE GRANDSON
OF CAPT. THOMAS
PEYTON II OF THE*
MEXICAN WAR
AND THE GREAT-
GRANDSON OF
CAPT. THOMAS WEST PEYTON
OF THE WAR OF 1812

38

GLASS CATFISH
The Orient
ITS TRANSPARENT BODY REVEALS ITS SPINE AND BONES WITH ASTOUNDING CLARITY

THE **REV. JOHN LIVINGSTON**
(1603 - 1672)
ANCESTOR OF THE FAMED LIVINGSTON FAMILY OF AMERICA
WAS THE FIRST SCOTTISH MINISTER TO CARRY A WATCH

THE **MOSQUE** of **SANGAR el GAWLY** in Cairo, Egypt,
HAS NOT HAD A SINGLE WINDOW PANE BROKEN IN **659** YEARS
NATIVES HAVE CAREFULLY GUARDED ITS GLASS WINDOWS SINCE 1304 IN THE BELIEF A SINGLE CRACKED PANE WOULD RESULT IN **AN EGYPTIAN DISASTER**

PIONEER KENTUCKIANS IN THE YEARS JUST PRIOR TO 1800 TREATED WINTER COLDS BY SPENDING A NIGHT OUTDOORS IN THE DEEP SNOW BEFORE A ROARING FIRE—AND DRINKING *A PINT OF BEAR FAT*

ANDREW HALL (1722-1808) of Kinfauns, Scotland, AND HIS FATHER AND GRANDFATHER SERVED SUCCESSIVELY AS PARISH GRAVEDIGGERS *FOR A CONTINUOUS PERIOD OF 160 YEARS*

A HUGE HOLLOW IDOL

WAS BUILT OF WICKER BY THE DRUIDS OF ANCIENT GAUL AND BRITAIN ON CERTAIN HOLIDAYS AND FILLED WITH CRIMINALS

—THEN SET ON FIRE!

THE FIRST MONEY

A COPPER INGOT MARKED "PURE" IN PHOENICIAN CHARACTERS *WAS USED AS CURRENCY IN THE 16th CENTURY B.C.*

RANNY SMETHERS

of Othello, Wash.,

ON THE SECOND HOLE AT MOSES LAKE GOLF CLUB *MADE A HOLE IN ONE* HIS FATHER SCORED A *BIRDIE 2* AND HIS BROTHER GREG HAD A *PAR 3*

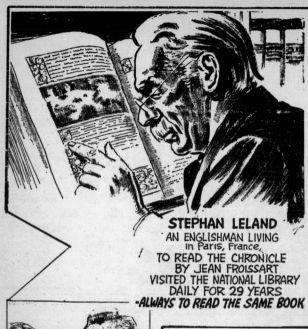

STEPHAN LELAND
AN ENGLISHMAN LIVING
in Paris, France,
TO READ THE CHRONICLE
BY JEAN FROISSART
VISITED THE NATIONAL LIBRARY
DAILY FOR 29 YEARS
-ALWAYS TO READ THE SAME BOOK

THE FRIENDLY EAGLE
NATURAL STONE FORMATION
RESEMBLING AN EAGLE
IN THE ACT OF KISSING
A YOUNG GIRL
near Nish, Yugoslavia

MEMORIAL TO A PUMP

"THIS OLD PUMP
NOW AT REST
STANDS AS A
MEMORIAL
TO THOSE IT
SERVED"

PLAQUE ON A PUMP PRESERVED
IN CEMETERY AT OAK CREEK, WIS.
Submitted by Anne Monson,
South Milwaukee, Wis.

JOHN MATTOCKS
WHO WAS ELECTED GOVERNOR of Vermont in 1843 *NEVER MADE A CAMPAIGN SPEECH* HIS ONLY CAMPAIGN PROMISE WAS A PLEDGE TO HAVE **2 THANKSGIVINGS EACH YEAR**

WRIST WATCH
THAT HAS KEPT PERFECT TIME *-WITHOUT EVER BEING REPAIRED, CLEANED OR OILED - FOR* **32 YEARS**

Owned by MISS CLAIRE SWEHLA
Cedar Rapids, Iowa

THE MOSQUE OF SAMPGAON
Bombay
HAD **$25,000** IN GOLD SOVEREIGNS
IN PLAIN VIEW ON ITS ROOF
FOR **43** YEARS
*THE GOVERNOR OF SAMPGAON LEFT THE
GOLD THERE IN 1829 AND IT WAS FORGOTTEN
UNTIL HIS WILL WAS READ IN 1872*

THE GREEN FROG
(Phyllomedusa Yhering)
of Brazil
LAYS ITS EGGS ABOVE
A STREAM IN A
LEAF IT HAS ROLLED
INTO THE SHAPE
OF A FUNNEL
*SO THE HATCHED
TADPOLES CAN
SLIP DIRECTLY
INTO THE WATER*

NATIVES of the Ubangi Territory, in Africa,
ALWAYS MOVE THEIR VILLAGE AFTER A CHIEF'S DEATH,
TRANSPORTING EACH HUT ON 3 CANOES ACROSS A RIVER

THE BLUE FROG
(Phyllomedusa bicolor) of Brazil

PROTECTS ITS EYES FROM MOSQUITO BITES *BY ROLLING ITS BULGING EYEBALLS INSIDE ITS MOUTH*

THE PRAYING BUDDHA
near Onseri, in the Diamond Mountains of Korea
NATURAL STONE FORMATION

The EIFFEL TOWER
in Paris, France, WAS "SOLD" TO A DUTCH SYNDICATE IN 1947 AS JUNK BY A VEGETABLE PEDDLER FOR $300,000

AND HE ACTUALLY COLLECTED A DOWN PAYMENT OF $150,000

– AND A 5-YEAR JAIL TERM

THE HEARTHSTONE
IN THE KITCHEN OF THE
BAY HORSE INN, Merrington, England,
ORIGINALLY WAS A
TOMBSTONE

THE **MAN** WHO HAD
**10,000
TOMBSTONES!**
KAN TANG
A CHINESE SCHOLAR
WHO SAVED HIS
EMPEROR FROM
ASSASSINATION
WAS SO REVERED FOR
HIS COURAGE THAT A
SPECIAL TOMBSTONE
ERECTED FOR HIM BY
THE GRATEFUL EMPEROR
*WAS DUPLICATED THROUGH-
OUT CHINA FOR 400 YEARS*

**KNEELING
ELEPHANT**
*NATURAL
STONE
FORMATION
IN PRILEP,
YUGOSLAVIA*

Submitted by
Stankovic Vladislav
Belgrade, Yugoslavia

46

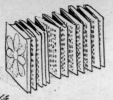

THE MAGICIANS' BOOK

RECORDING THE SECRETS OF BATAK MAGICIANS of Indonesia

CONSISTS OF PAGES MADE FROM THE INNER BARK OF A TREE, AND THE INK, MADE FROM SOOT, *PERIODICALLY VANISHES*

LEWIS CROOKALL

of Blackpool, England, TO ATTEND A MEETING OF THE PRESTON GUILD, WALKED FROM BLACKPOOL TO PRESTON AND BACK - A DISTANCE OF **40 MILES** - *AT THE AGE OF 91*

THE CHAPEL of TRANSTAMARE

in the Cathedral of Cordoba, Spain, CANNOT BE ENTERED BECAUSE IT WAS BUILT HIGH UP ON ONE WALL OF THE CATHEDRAL - *AND NO STAIRWAY LEADS TO IT*

HANS WIESENJAGGL A POACHER of Kaltenbrunn, Austria, ILLEGALLY KILLED 1,300 CHAMOIS —YET HE WAS PARDONED BECAUSE HE HAD PLEDGED TO HIS DYING FATHER THAT HE WOULD RETIRE AFTER BAGGING HIS 1,300th CHAMOIS

WOMEN of Novi, Yugoslavia, STILL WEAR MOURNING FOR PETER ZRINY AND FRANZ FRANKOPAN WHO WERE HANGED ON FALSE CHARGES OF TREASON 294 YEARS AGO

"**KING TUT WAS MURDERED,**"
SAYS J. CARTER BROWN, DIRECTOR OF THE NATIONAL
GALLERY OF ART. BUT FURTHER INTRIGUE
SURROUNDS TUT WHOSE BURIAL VAULT
BEARS THE INSCRIPTION:"*DEATH WILL
COME SWIFTLY TO THOSE
WHO DISTURB THE CONTENTS!*"
12 PEOPLE WHO HELPED UNCOVER THE
TOMB HAVE SINCE MET
MYSTERIOUS DEATHS !

THE **SHIP** THAT SOUNDED
ITS OWN DIRGE
THE "ATLANTIC", WRECKED
OFF FISHER'S ISLAND,
in Long Island Sound
WAS POUNDED TO BITS ON
THE ROCKY SHORE
-YET ITS BELL CONTINUED
TO FLOAT ON SUPPORTING
TIMBERS **AND PEALED
ON FOR DAYS** (1846)

THE FIRST TWO NAMES OF
ANNA EDE PASKERVILLE
READ THE SAME *FORWARD*
AND BACKWARD
Manchester, Iowa

**CAPTAIN
ETHAN
CLARKE**
(1745-1833)
MUSTERED OUT
OF THE FIRST
RHODE ISLAND
REGIMENT AFTER THE
AMERICAN REVOLUTION,
*CONTINUED TO WEAR
HIS UNIFORM DAILY*
FOR THE NEXT 50 YEARS

THE
**SINGAPORE
HOLLY**
IS NOT FROM
SINGAPORE - NOR
IS IT A HOLLY
*IT IS A NETTLE
-AND FROM THE*
West Indies

THE **GROUND MULLET,** THE **GULF KINGFISH** AND THE **SOUTHERN WHITING** ARE THE SAME FISH

DICK WILLIAMS of Scottsdale, Arizona, WON RINGS AND PARALLEL-BAR CHAMPIONSHIPS IN STATEWIDE COMPETITIONS -YET HIS LEFT LEG WAS CRIPPLED BY POLIO AND HAD TO BE KEPT STRAPPED TO HIS OTHER LEG

Children of the Madi Tribe, in Uganda, Africa, HAVING NEITHER CLASSROOMS NOR SLATES, USE THE OPEN DESERT AS THEIR SCHOOLHOUSE **AND WRITE THEIR LESSONS IN THE SAND**

CRAB ORCHARD STONE
A SANDSTONE QUARRIED in Cumberland County, Tenn.,
IS SO HARD THAT
IT CAN CUT GLASS

HOMERO BLANCAS
of Houston University, Texas,
PLAYING ON THE PAR 70 PREMIER GOLF COURSE near Longview, Texas,
IN TOURNAMENT COMPETITION PLAYED THE LAST 18 HOLES IN ONLY 55 STROKES
HIS LAST 2 ROUNDS WERE 62-55 FOR 117
A WORLD'S RECORD FOR 36 HOLES
August 1962

THE **YELLOW** BIRD'S NEST
a plant
GROWS WITHOUT SUNLIGHT AND IS UNABLE TO MANUFACTURE ITS OWN FOOD
-BUT ITS ROOTS ARE COVERED WITH A FUNGUS WHICH ENABLES IT TO EXTRACT NOURISHMENT FROM DECAYED LEAVES IN THE SOIL

THE **HUTS** BUILT BY SHEPHERDS in Luberon, France, CONSIST MERELY OF LOOSE STONES WITHOUT MORTAR *-EXACTLY AS THEY WERE BUILT IN THE SAME LOCALITY* **THOUSANDS OF YEARS AGO**

THE **LAZIEST** RULER IN HISTORY
GIAN GASTONE (1671-1737)
LAST MEMBER OF THE MEDICI FAMILY,
WAS IN PERFECT HEALTH,
YET HE GOVERNED FLORENCE, ITALY,
FOR 8 YEARS **FROM HIS BED**

THE SPRAY CARBURETOR
OF THE FIRST AMERICAN CAR WAS ADAPTED BY CHARLES DURYEA FROM HIS WIFE'S *PERFUME ATOMIZER* 1892

OPTICAL ILLUSION
IS IT A HEXAGON OR A CUBE?
Submitted by ROBERT TOWNSEND Rumford, Me.

THE CORPSE THAT RULED ETHIOPIA

EMPEROR MENELIK II
DIED ON SEPT. 10, 1911

BUT FOR 2 YEARS, 3 MONTHS AND 2 DAYS *HE WAS STILL CONSIDERED THE REIGNING MONARCH BY ALL HIS SUBJECTS*

THE MUSIC-LOVING BULL OF INGS
England
WHEN A RADIO BRINGS IT THE SOUND OF MUSIC
THE BULL STAMPS ITS FEET AND DANCES IN TIME WITH THE MUSIC

THE **OFFICIAL SOBRIETY TEST**

IN SOME RURAL COMMUNITIES in Italy

REQUIRES THE SUSPECT TO PERFORM **A DANCE**

THE **SENTENCE** HANDED DOWN BY JUDGES IN 18th CENTURY CENTRAL EUROPE AGAINST A MEMBER OF THE COBBLERS' GUILD WAS IN THE FORM OF A DRAWING OF A COBBLER'S BENCH -WITH THE NUMBER OF BLOWS TO BE ADMINISTERED FOR EACH OFFENSE FORMING AN ADDITIONAL LEG TO THE BENCH

LEMON *SHAPED LIKE AN OCTOPUS* Submitted by CARL THOMPSON San Mateo, Calif.

SLOWE GOING and WAITE WORK TOGETHER IN NEW YORK CITY

THE FISH THAT CATCH THEMSELVES

MULLET ATTEMPTING TO RETURN TO THE MEDITERRANEAN WHEN THE SUMMER SUN HEATS THE WATERS OF LAKE BARDAWIL ARE CAUGHT IN HORIZONTAL NETS *INTO WHICH THE FRANTIC FISH LEAP BY THE HUNDREDS OF THOUSANDS* (Sinai Peninsula)

PRINCESS BREEZEWOOD R·A·PATSY A HOLSTEIN- FRIESIAN COW of Vienna, Ohio, *IN A PERIOD OF ONE YEAR PRODUCED* 1,866 POUNDS OF BUTTERFAT

CRICKET FIGHTS

STAGED BY THE CHINESE ARE ATTENDED BY HUGE CROWDS AND THE CONTENDERS ARE DIVIDED INTO CLASSES —FIGHTING AS **HEAVYWEIGHTS, MIDDLEWEIGHTS OR LIGHTWEIGHTS** *THE WINNER MUST CHIRP AFTER ITS VICTORY —OR IT IS DISQUALIFIED*

ADELAIDE HOCHE
(1776 - 1859)

WHOSE HUSBAND, FRENCH GENERAL LAZARE HOCHE, DIED IN 1799, REMAINED A WIDOW FOR 60 YEARS

HAVING REJECTED MARRIAGE PROPOSALS FROM 3 FRENCH FIELD MARSHALS - ONE OF WHOM, BERNADOTTE, BECAME KING OF SWEDEN

QUEEN SALOTE

THE **BLANKETS** WORN BY NATIVES OF the Tonga Islands, in the South Pacific, ARE ADORNED BY A CRUDE DESIGN OF A PLANE -A REMINDER THAT THE ISLANDERS CONTRIBUTED A SPITFIRE BEARING THEIR QUEEN'S NAME TO THE BRITISH IN WORLD WAR II

A **BEER BARREL**

3½ FEET HIGH, SHAPED LIKE A BEER MUG, AND FORMERLY USED BY KINGS OF PRUSSIA, IS COMPLETELY COVERED WITH *HUNDREDS OF SILVER DOLLARS*

KING DHANA NANDA

of Magadha, India, WAS ONE OF 8 BROTHERS WHO RULED THE COUNTRY SUCCESSIVELY FOR A PERIOD OF ONLY 12 YEARS

-EACH SUFFERING A VIOLENT DEATH !

(338 - 326 B.C.)

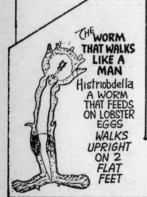

The WORM THAT WALKS LIKE A MAN

Histriobdella A WORM THAT FEEDS ON LOBSTER EGGS *WALKS UPRIGHT ON 2 FLAT FEET*

AN **EXACT REPLICA OF THE GROTTO** of **LOURDES** in the Botanic Garden of Yanam, India, CONSTRUCTED BY AN AMERICAN ENGINEER IN 1944 WHEN HE RE-FLOATED A 1,000-TON SHIP AFTER A PRAYER *• ALTHOUGH IT HAD REMAINED FIRMLY WEDGED ON A ROCKY SHELF THROUGH A FULL YEAR OF LABOR*

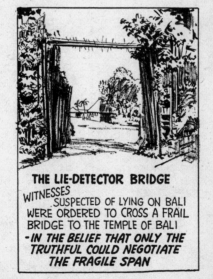

THE LIE-DETECTOR BRIDGE

WITNESSES SUSPECTED OF LYING ON BALI WERE ORDERED TO CROSS A FRAIL BRIDGE TO THE TEMPLE OF BALI *• IN THE BELIEF THAT ONLY THE TRUTHFUL COULD NEGOTIATE THE FRAGILE SPAN*

A **PERSIAN CAT** OWNED BY THE ITALIAN DUKE OF SPOLETO WAS GIVEN THE ROYAL NAME OF TOMISLAW II TO SHOW ITS OWNER'S DISAPPROVAL OF MUSSOLINI'S ACTION IN NAMING THE DUKE TO BE KING TOMISLAW II OF CROATIA

THE **ELABORATELY CARVED DOORWAYS** in Mukalla, Arabia, ARE CONSIDERED SO IMPORTANT THAT THEY ARE USUALLY ERECTED FIRST — AND THEN A HOUSE IS **BUILT AROUND THEM**

THE **CECROPIA TREES** of So. America HAVE **HOLLOW STEMS** **WHICH SERVE AS NESTS FOR FEROCIOUS ANTS**

THE LANTERN PUFFBALL a fungus HAS OPENINGS THAT MAKE IT LOOK LIKE A PLASTIC PRACTICE GOLF BALL

THE LEANING MINARET of AGRA India SLANTS 16 INCHES OUT OF THE VERTICAL

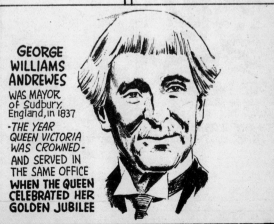

GEORGE WILLIAMS ANDREWES WAS MAYOR of Sudbury, England, in 1837 -THE YEAR QUEEN VICTORIA WAS CROWNED- AND SERVED IN THE SAME OFFICE WHEN THE QUEEN CELEBRATED HER GOLDEN JUBILEE

PADDY, THE RAM
A CHARACTER OF SYDNEY, AUSTRALIA, IN SUMMER AND WINTER
ALWAYS WORE 2 COATS, 4 SHIRTS AND 3 PAIRS OF TROUSERS

THE
REV. M.
HOYT
of Beadle
County, S.D.,
IN 55
YEARS
AS A
MINISTER
*BUILT
25
CHURCHES*

BUTTERNUT SQUASH
SHAPED LIKE
A SWAN

Grown by
ROBERT TREAT
Woodmont, Conn.

DUKE LOUIS de La TRÉMOILLE
(1838-1911) of France
DIED 120 YEARS AFTER THE DEATH OF HIS SISTER—
THE DUKE'S SISTER, CAROLINE, DIED AT THE AGE OF 2
-47 YEARS BEFORE THE BIRTH OF HER BROTHER

A MONUMENT TO BEEFSTEW
THE ORNATE MONUMENT in Carpentras, France, SHOWING A DISH COOKING OVER A BLAZING FIRE *COMMEMORATES POT-AU-FEU -- A TYPICAL FRENCH STEW*

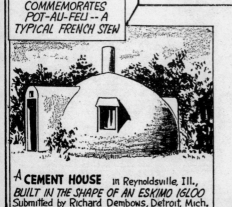

A **CEMENT HOUSE** in Reynoldsville, Ill., *BUILT IN THE SHAPE OF AN ESKIMO IGLOO*
Submitted by Richard Dembows, Detroit, Mich.

from an old print

THE WINE CASKS THAT WON A WAR!

DUKE ALEXANDER FARNESE CONQUERED ANTWERP, BELGIUM, BY FLOATING HIS ARTILLERY ACROSS THE RIVER SCHELDE *ON RAFTS SUPPORTED BY WINE BARRELS* (1585)

THE NEST

of the MOSQUITO BEE of the Straits Settlements, Malaysia, IS BUILT WITH A NARROW APPROACH PASSAGE

SO IT CAN BE MORE EASILY GUARDED AGAINST ATTACK

THE MOST ELABORATE BARN DOOR IN ALL BRITAIN

Newhall, England

A MAGNIFICENT DOORWAY WAS DESIGNED BY JAMES MOORE FOR A NEW HOME IN THE 17th CENTURY, BUT LITIGATION OVER THE PROPERTY USED UP ALL HIS FUNDS

-SO HE MADE IT THE ENTRANCE TO HIS BARN

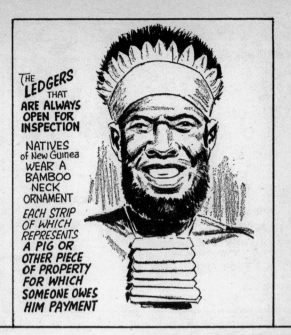

THE **LEDGERS** THAT **ARE ALWAYS OPEN FOR INSPECTION**

NATIVES of New Guinea **WEAR A BAMBOO NECK ORNAMENT** *EACH STRIP OF WHICH REPRESENTS A PIG OR OTHER PIECE OF PROPERTY FOR WHICH SOMEONE OWES HIM PAYMENT*

SERGIUS A MONK in the monastery of Djebel el Tair, Egypt, **BLESSED EVERY SHIP PASSING UP OR DOWN THE NILE BY SWIMMING TO THEM WITH HIS CLOTHING BALANCED ON HIS HEAD** *-YET IN 31 YEARS HIS GARMENTS NEVER ONCE TOUCHED THE WATER!*

FISHERMEN
of the Cofan Tribe, in Colombia,
KILL THEIR CATCH BY
BITING EACH FISH'S NECK

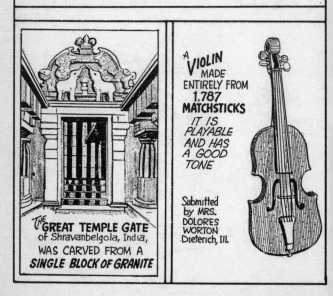

THE **GREAT TEMPLE GATE**
of Shravanbelgola, India,
WAS CARVED FROM A
SINGLE BLOCK OF GRANITE

A **VIOLIN**
MADE
ENTIRELY FROM
1,787
MATCHSTICKS
IT IS
PLAYABLE
AND HAS
A GOOD
TONE

Submitted
by MRS.
DOLORES
WORTON
Dieterich, Ill.

SIR JOHN PRYCE
(1698-1761)
of Newtown, Wales.

GRIEF STRICKEN BY THE DEATH
OF HIS WIFE, ELIZABETH,
*KEPT HER EMBALMED BODY IN THE
BEDROOM FOR 11 YEARS -EVEN AFTER HE HAD
TAKEN MARY MORRIS AS HIS 2nd WIFE*
WHEN MARY DIED HE HAD HER EMBALMED
BODY INSTALLED IN HIS BEDCHAMBER ALSO
·BUT HE DISPOSED OF BOTH BODIES AT
THE INSISTENCE OF HIS THIRD WIFE

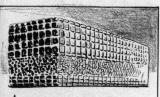

A **COFFIN**, FOUND IN
Massarah, Egypt, in 1888
WAS MADE FROM THE ENTIRE
HIDE OF A CROCODILE

THE **CALIFORNIAN BLIND GOBY**

LIVES IN CREVICES
IN ROCKS ON
THE SHORE

THE **KNEELING SATYR** in the Theatre of Dionysos, Greece, WAS GIVEN THE FACE OF SOCRATES BECAUSE ALCIBIADES, A PUPIL OF SOCRATES, 500 YEARS EARLIER SAID HIS MASTER RESEMBLED *"A DRUNKEN POT-BELLIED SATYR"*

THE **GRAND DUCHESS DETCHIN WANGMO** ruler of Kanze, Tibet, HAS BEEN DIVORCED *25 TIMES*

E.O. SAUNDERS of Pomeroy, Ohio, TAUGHT SCHOOL IN 3 STATES -OHIO, W.VIRGINIA AND KENTUCKY- *FOR A TOTAL OF 63 YEARS*

KING RADAMA II
of Madagascar
WAS ASSASSINATED
WHEN HE ABOLISHED
ALL POLICE FORCES AND
RULED THAT ALL DISPUTES
BETWEEN INDIVIDUALS
AND MUNICIPALITIES
MUST BE SETTLED
BY DUELS (1863)

THE OLDEST HOUSE IN BRAZIL
A DWELLING in Parahyba, Brazil,
*USED CONTINUOUSLY
FOR 365 YEARS*

A GIANT SQUARE JELLYFISH

WHICH DWELLS DEEP IN THE OCEAN

OFTEN IS THE NURSERY FOR **350** FISH

THE **SIGNATURE** OF MAURICE PHILIP the French poet WHOSE LAST NAME MEANS *"HORSE FANCIER"*

GENERAL AUGUSTE COLBERT (1777-1809)

FIGHTING WITH NAPOLEON'S FORCES in the battle of Wagram, Austria, IN 1809, WAS HIT BY A BULLET THAT ENTERED NEAR HIS RIGHT EAR AND EMERGED THROUGH HIS LEFT EAR *-YET HE WAS NOT EVEN HOSPITALIZED!*

DOCTORS FOUND THAT THE BULLET HAD DETOURED INSIDE HIS SKULL AND HAD NOT DONE THE SLIGHTEST HARM

William FITZHARDING
(1785-1857)

WAS MADE EARL of FITZHARDING AS A REWARD FOR HIS EFFORTS IN GETTING *ALL FOUR OF HIS BROTHERS ELECTED TO THE BRITISH PARLIAMENT IN THE SAME YEAR* (1841)

THE **LEANING TOWER OF JIDDAH**

A MINARET in Saudi Arabia THAT IS TILTING *15 INCHES OUT OF LINE*

JAMES ISHERWOOD
AN INNKEEPER IN Haslingden, England, TO WIN A WAGER

ATE 20 RAW EGGS IN 7 MINUTES -INCLUDING THEIR SHELLS

71

MRS. TWILA STEED
of Leachville, Ark.,

IS THE MOTHER
OF 4 SONS
*ALL BORN ON
OCT. 27th IN
DIFFERENT YEARS*

THE **WATCH TOWER**
of the
MEDIEVAL
FORTRESS OF
ST. MICHAEL,
on Malta
HAS A
HUMAN
EYE AND
EAR
CARVED
ON ITS
SIDES
-TO AID
IT IN
DETECTING
SURPRISE
ATTACKS

MRS. JOHN B. KIRBY
AND HER DAUGHTER,
MRS. MALCOLM KING,
members of the Pine
Orchard Y. and C.C.,
Branford, Conn.,
BOTH MADE HOLES-IN-
ONE ON THE SAME
HOLE DURING THE
SAME WEEK END
July, 1963

GR-R-R-R

A **BULLDOG** owned by
Ludwig Hausing, manager of the
City Theatre, Glogau, Germany,
WAS NAMED "ADVANCE"
-AND TRAINED TO GROWL
OMINOUSLY WHEN ITS
NAME WAS MENTIONED
-TO DISCOURAGE ACTORS
FROM ASKING FOR AN
ADVANCE ON THEIR PAY

Here lyes the Body
Robt R

Robt. RUSSAL
(1744-1771)

A STONE-CUTTER OF Newtownards, Ireland, CARVED HIS OWN EPITAPH ON A PILLAR IN THE LOCAL ABBEY WHEN HE WAS SEEMINGLY IN PERFECT HEALTH AND ONLY 27 YEARS OF AGE

-YET HE DIED OF NATURAL CAUSES AND WAS BURIED BESIDE THE PILLAR ONLY A FEW DAYS LATER

COINS USED IN 18th CENTURY MEXICO WERE MINTED IN THE SHAPE OF LEAVES

QUE VAS

THE BAPTISMAL FONT used for centuries in the Cathedral of Metz, France, WAS ORIGINALLY A BATHTUB *SALVAGED FROM AN ANCIENT ROMAN PUBLIC BATH*

Dr. **JULIUS TOWLER**
(1811-1886)
of HOBART COLLEGE,
Geneva, N.Y.,
SIMULTANEOUSLY TAUGHT

MATHEMATICS
PHILOSOPHY
CHEMISTRY
ANATOMY
PHYSIOLOGY
MODERN LANGUAGES
AND MEDICINE

OWLS HAVE BUILT IN
"WINDSHIELD WIPERS"

THE **FOOTPRINTS** of the **MADONNA**
WHERE THE MOTHER OF JESUS
STOOD AS HE PASSED ON
THE WAY TO CALVARY, ARE
OUTLINED IN MOSAIC ON
THE ROADWAY IN JERUSALEM

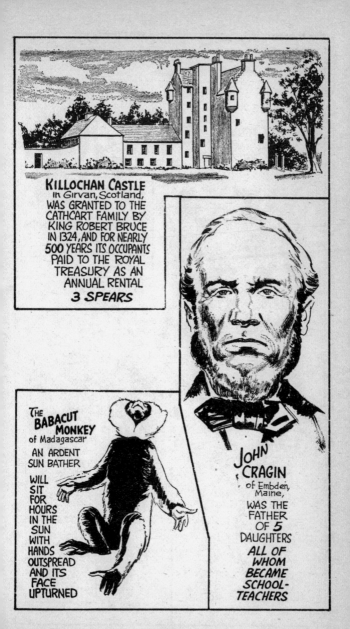

KILLOCHAN CASTLE in Girvan, Scotland, WAS GRANTED TO THE CATHCART FAMILY BY KING ROBERT BRUCE IN 1324, AND FOR NEARLY 500 YEARS ITS OCCUPANTS PAID TO THE ROYAL TREASURY AS AN ANNUAL RENTAL *3 SPEARS*

THE **BABACUT MONKEY** of Madagascar

AN ARDENT SUN BATHER

WILL SIT FOR HOURS IN THE SUN WITH HANDS OUTSPREAD AND ITS FACE UPTURNED

JOHN CRAGIN of Embden, Maine, WAS THE FATHER OF *5* DAUGHTERS *ALL OF WHOM BECAME SCHOOL-TEACHERS*

DR. W.M. MAC NEILL of Lillington, N.C., MARRIED A GIRL WHOSE BIRTH HE HAD ATTENDED *40 YEARS BEFORE*

THE SAND HILL DWELLINGS of the Amitermes termites of Panama ARE PALATIAL STRUCTURES

WHERE DO I VOTE?

NO MAN IN COLONIAL VIRGINIA WAS ENTITLED TO VOTE *UNLESS HE OWNED A CLOCK*

A WILLOW TREE in Baldwinsville, N.Y., GREW FROM THE RIDING CROP OF MRS. JONAS C. BALDWIN *WHICH SHE HAD STUCK INTO THE GROUND*

THE ALASKAN BLACKFISH
IS SO HARDY IT SUFFERS
NO HARM AFTER BEING
*FROZEN SOLID IN ICE FOR
A PERIOD OF WEEKS*

THE SOUND OF DOOM !
THE WHISTLE INSTALLED ON THE
S.S. TELL CITY, at West Point, Ky., ALSO
SERVED IN TURN THE S.S. EUGENE, THE
PACKET HETTIE GILMORE, THE S.S.
TARASCON AND THE PACKET SOUTHLAND
*-EVERY ONE OF WHICH WAS
DESTROYED BY FIRE OR SHIPWRECK*

ARAB WOMEN
MAY STOOP AT THEIR WORK
*-BUT ARE FORBIDDEN
TO KNEEL*

THE
**TAIL
OF THE
PORCUPINE**
WAS USED
BY THE
CROW INDIANS
AS A COMB

THE BONY BEARD OF THE WHALE IS USED BY NATIVES OF FIRELAND, IN So. America **AS A HAIR COMB**

THE SVOBODNIKI A RUSSIAN SECT of British Columbia **EAT NO MEAT, EGGS, FOWL OR DAIRY PRODUCTS, DRINK NO MILK, USE NEITHER LEATHER NOR WOOL AND DO ALL THEIR OWN WORK** IT IS AGAINST THEIR RELIGIOUS PRINCIPLES TO MAKE USE OF **ANY ANIMAL'S LABOR OR PRODUCT**

"THE POEM HOUSE" near Stutzerbach, Germany, IS SO CALLED BECAUSE THE FAMED POET, GOETHE, WROTE *"The Night Song of the Wanderer"* ON ONE OF THE BUILDING'S WOODEN WALLS

THE REV. THOMAS M. ALLEN of Paris, Ky., OFFERED THE NOMINATION FOR U.S. CONGRESS, DECLINED ON THE GROUNDS THAT IT WOULD *SET A BAD EXAMPLE FOR YOUNG MINISTERS*

AN ASSAULT TRIAL

WAS HELD IN THE COURT OF ASSIZES In Donegal, Ireland,

IN WHICH THE PLAINTIFF, THE DEFENDANT, THE PRESIDING JUSTICE, THE COURT CLERK, BOTH ATTORNEYS AND THE 3 WITNESSES *ALL WERE NAMED DOHERTY*

(1835)

THE ISLAND THAT NEVER STANDS STILL!
MERCURY ISLAND
in the South Atlantic
IS SO HONEYCOMBED WITH TUNNELS
THAT THE POUNDING SEAS CAUSE IT TO
QUIVER LIKE QUICKSILVER!

A MICROCALORIMETER
INVENTED BY PROFESSOR E. CALVET
and used at the University of Montreal
*CAN MEASURE THE TEMPERATURE
OF A FLY'S BREATH*

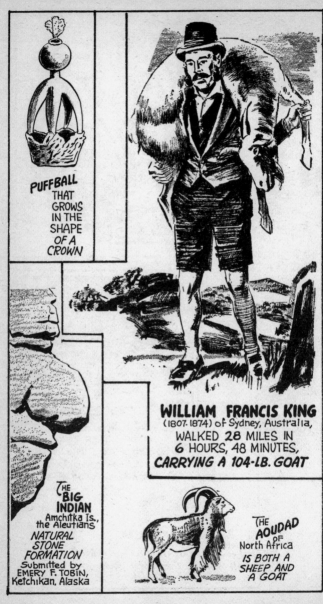

PUFFBALL THAT GROWS IN THE SHAPE OF A CROWN

THE BIG INDIAN
Amchitka Is., the Aleutians
NATURAL STONE FORMATION
Submitted by EMERY F. TOBIN, Ketchikan, Alaska

WILLIAM FRANCIS KING
(1807-1874) of Sydney, Australia,
WALKED 28 MILES IN 6 HOURS, 48 MINUTES, CARRYING A 104-LB. GOAT

THE AOUDAD OF North Africa IS BOTH A SHEEP AND A GOAT

DIONYSIUS
(431 B.C.–367 B.C.)
the tyrant of Syracuse

ALWAYS HAD HIS HAIR AND BEARD TRIMMED WITH RED-HOT COALS!

HE WAS SO FEARFUL OF ASSASSINATION THAT HE NEVER PERMITTED A RAZOR OR SCISSORS NEAR HIS THROAT

THE **CANOES** of the Sanapana Indians of the Gran Chaco, S.A., ARE MADE FROM THE TRUNKS OF THE BOTTLE TREE, THE WOOD OF WHICH IS SO SOFT IT CAN BE SCOOPED OUT WITH SPADES **–YET THE BARK IS AS HARD AS IRON**

THE **250,000 TURKISH SOLDIERS** WHO FOUGHT THE RUSSIANS IN 1877 -WORE SILK SHIRTS IN BATTLE IN THE BELIEF THAT SINCE SILK DOES NOT TEAR EASILY *A BULLET COULD BE EXTRACTED FROM A WOUND MERELY BY YANKING AT THE SHIRT*

THE **HIGHEST LIGHTHOUSE IN THE WORLD** OLD POINT LOMA LIGHTHOUSE in San Diego County, Calif., WHICH WAS OPERATED UNTIL 1891 *IS 510 FEET ABOVE SEA LEVEL*

THE **PALACE** OF THE **TURKISH GOVERNOR** in Riadh, capital of Saudi Arabia, TO DEMONSTRATE THE PRESENT GOVERNMENT'S SCORN FOR THE TURKS, *WAS CONVERTED INTO A PRISON*

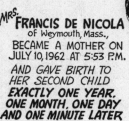

MRS. **FRANCIS DE NICOLA**
of Weymouth, Mass.,
BECAME A MOTHER ON
JULY 10, 1962 AT 5:53 P.M.

AND GAVE BIRTH TO
HER SECOND CHILD
*EXACTLY ONE YEAR,
ONE MONTH, ONE DAY
AND ONE MINUTE LATER*

THE
REV. ROBERT QUARTERMAN
(1787-1849) of Midway, Ga.,
SAW HIS 4 SONS BECOME
MINISTERS -AND MARRIED
*HIS 2 DAUGHTERS
TO MINISTERS*

THE
**STARFISH
FLOWER**
(Stapelia gigantea)
of South Africa
LOOKS LIKE A
STARFISH ENWRAPPED
IN WEEDS

POLICE CHIEF **BYRON PARRISH** of Ranger, Texas, FAMED AS A PISTOL SHOT COULD THROW A CAN INTO THE AIR AND HIT IT **12** TIMES -FIRING SIMULTANEOUSLY WITH **2** SIX-SHOOTERS

THE **HAIRY FROG** of Africa IS COVERED WITH *FUR*

(Trichobatrachus robustus)

84

THE **GENTLEMAN OF THE MOUNTAINS**
NATURAL STONE FORMATION
Elkhorn Mountain,
Hardy County, W.Va.

The
PEAL
of
PEACE

LAKE VÄTTER— in Sweden
DEVELOPS HIGH WAVES
ON THE CALMEST DAYS
*WHENEVER WIND WHIPS UP
LAKE CONSTANCE, in Switzerland,*
1,200 MILES AWAY

THE BELL OF ROVERETO— *Italy*
WHICH IS RUNG TO OBSERVE
MEMORIAL DAYS THROUGHOUT
THE WORLD WAS CAST FROM THE
CANNON OF EVERY NATION THAT
FOUGHT IN WORLD WAR I
—BOTH FRIEND AND FOE

THE PROPHECY THAT TRICKED ITS VICTIM —

PRINCE JOZEF PONIATOWSKI
(1763-1813)
of Poland
AVOIDED BIRDS ALL HIS LIFE BECAUSE A GYPSY WARNED THAT HE WOULD BE **KILLED BY A MAGPIE**

THE PRINCE WAS DROWNED CROSSING GERMANY'S ELSTER RIVER

"ELSTER" IN GERMAN MEANS "MAGPIE"

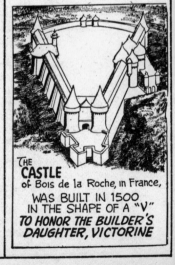

THE CASTLE
of Bois de la Roche, in France,
WAS BUILT IN 1500 IN THE SHAPE OF A "V"
TO HONOR THE BUILDER'S DAUGHTER, VICTORINE

THE MAN WHO RETURNED TO HAUNT THE COURT THAT TOOK HIS LIFE!

OSWALD KRÖL of Lindau, Germany, WAS CONVICTED OF MURDER AND EXECUTED! KRÖL WAS LATER VINDICATED —AND FOR 50 YEARS HIS SKELETON STOOD BEFORE THE JURIST WHO HAD PRONOUNCED THE DEATH SENTENCE!

GABES in the Tunisian Sahara, beside the Mediterranean, IS THE ONLY OASIS IN THE WORLD *LOCATED ON THE SEASHORE*

A **MONUMENT** ON A ROAD IN PERU BETWEEN LIMA AND CALLAO IS TOPPED BY A WRECKED AUTO AND BEARS THE INSCRIPTION: *"THE SLOWER YOU TRAVEL THE FURTHER YOU'LL JOURNEY"*

John MCKEOWN A HERMIT of Dixie, Idaho, *ALWAYS WORE 6 SUITS ONE OVER ANOTHER* — AND CARRIED MONEY IN THE POCKETS OF EACH SUIT HE DIED OF A COLD AFTER AUTHORITIES FORCED HIM TO TAKE HIS FIRST BATH

Mrs. **RAY C. SCHOENHERR** of Detroit, Mich., IS THE MOTHER OF 7 CHILDREN

JEANNETTE, BORN ON A **MONDAY**
KATHLEEN, BORN ON A **TUESDAY**
SUZANNE, BORN ON A **WEDNESDAY**
ANDREW, BORN ON A **THURSDAY**
THOMAS, BORN ON A **FRIDAY**
MARY, BORN ON A **SATURDAY**
JOSEPH, BORN ON A **SUNDAY**

COUNT ALEXIS BESTUZHEV-RIUMIN

(1695-1766) of Russia
A DIPLOMAT FOR HALF A CENTURY,
ROSE TO BECOME CHANCELLOR
OF THE RUSSIAN EMPIRE
*BECAUSE HE MUMBLED SO BADLY
HE COULD ALWAYS CLAIM HE
HAD BEEN MISUNDERSTOOD*

HANDMADE ALMANACS

WERE WORN
SUSPENDED FROM
A CHAIN BY
14th CENTURY
ENGLISH
HOUSEWIVES AS
*A REMINDER
OF WHEN TO
PERFORM*
DOMESTIC CHORES

THE CAPERCAILLE

CAN ONLY BE CAUGHT
WHILE IT GOBBLES

MELCHIOR KHLESL
(1552-1630)
of Vienna, Austria,

WHO FELT PRAYER HAD CURED HIM OF LEPROSY

PRAYED IN THE SAME CHURCH EVERY DAY THEREAFTER FOR 53 YEARS

THE HOUSE THAT COMPRISES AN ENTIRE VILLAGE
TAGADIRT
in the Atlas Mountains of Morocco
HAS A POPULATION OF 1,001 PERSONS
-ALL OF WHOM LIVE IN A SINGLE TERRACED STRUCTURE

90

THE **HUMAN PINCUSHION**

CAPT. LEWIS KRAATZ
(1773-1858) of Independence, Texas, WAS LEFT FOR DEAD ON THE PRAIRIE BY INDIANS —WITH 27 ARROWS IN HIS BODY—

HE RECOVERED AND LIVED ANOTHER 18 YEARS

THE **"WEDDING RING"** OF ARAMIA TRIBESMEN; OF NEW GUINEA, IS A ***CONICAL CAP DONNED ON THEIR WEDDING DAY.*** *THE HAIR GROWS THROUGH THE MESH AND MAKES IT IMPOSSIBLE TO REMOVE THE CAP*

JACOB BURVIN FUNKHOUSER
of Hambleton, W.Va.,
TO PAY OFF AN ELECTION BET
IN 1936 CRAWLED FROM HAMBLETON
TO PARSONS, A DISTANCE OF 2 MILES,
IN 3½ HOURS – *ALTHOUGH HE
WAS 60 YEARS OF AGE*

BIRD IN ITS BATH
NATURAL ROCK FORMATION
in the Enchanted Valley, Argentina

WILLIAM MARGRAVE
of Fort Scott,
Kansas,
SIMULTANEOUSLY
SERVED AS
*JUSTICE OF
THE PEACE
CLERK OF
THE COURT
PROBATE
JUDGE*
AND *POLICE
JUSTICE*

RABBITS CAN RUN FASTER *UPHILL THAN DOWN*

THE DUKE OF CAXIAS (1803-1880) FAMED SOLDIER AND STATESMAN *WAS THE ONLY BRAZILIAN DUKE IN THE COUNTRY'S HISTORY*

OSKAR FRANZ (1885-1956) CARRYING **44** POUNDS OF BRICKS IN A PACK CLIMBED MT. HOCHSCHWAB, in AUSTRIA, TO ITS **7,500**-FOOT-HIGH PEAK *297 TIMES -JUST FOR EXERCISE*

KARL DEWEY MYERS (1899-1951)
who became Poet Laureate
of West Virginia
WAS A CRIPPLE WHO NEVER WEIGHED
MORE THAN 60 POUNDS AND
WAS COMPLETELY SELF-EDUCATED
*HE MEMORIZED THE DECLARATION
OF INDEPENDENCE, THE CONSTITUTION
OF THE U.S., THE MAYFLOWER COMPACT
AND THE MAGNA CHARTA*

THE **STRANGEST CHRISTMAS SHOPPING IN THE WORLD**

THE **NIGHT** OF **RADISHES**
A MARKET SET UP IN Oaxaca, Mexico, EACH CHRISTMAS EVE SELLS ONLY RADISHES -BUT EACH ONE IS MADE TO LOOK LIKE A PERSON OR ANIMAL

THE LLOG
A CROSS BETWEEN
A LLAMA AND A DOG

THE **NEST**
OF THE MASON BEE
IS CONSTRUCTED
INSIDE THE WHORLS
OF *AN ABANDONED
SNAIL SHELL*

SANTA CLAUS
AS THE FAT, JOLLY, RED-CHEEKED,
WHITE-WHISKERED, UNIVERSALLY
RECOGNIZED ST. NICK, WAS CREATED
BY CARTOONIST THOMAS NAST
OVER 100 YEARS AGO!

A **PORTABLE** SUN DIAL
USED IN 18th CENTURY
ENGLAND, WAS SHAPED
LIKE A NAPKIN RING
–*A RAY OF LIGHT PASSING THROUGH
AN APERTURE TO ILLUMINATE
MARKINGS INSIDE THE RING*

95

THE OLD TOLL BRIDGE between New York and City Island
WAS BUILT IN 1873 WITH TIMBER SALVAGED FROM
THE 90-GUN BATTLESHIP NORTH CAROLINA

THE
CONUS SNAIL
of the South Pacific
IS SO POISONOUS
THAT ITS BITE
CAN KILL A MAN

KING WENZEL (1361-1419)
of Germany
WAS SO POVERTY STRICKEN
*THAT TO FEED HIMSELF AND
HIS COURT HE OFTEN
HOCKED HIS CROWN*

A DUGOUT CANOE
IN USE CONSTANTLY ON
Lake Walchen, Bavaria,
FOR 210 YEARS

THE **NEST** of
Brazilian wasps
IS A CARDBOARD
DRUM *MANUFACTURED
BY THE WASPS
FROM WOODPULP*

THE
MAN WHOSE LIFE BEGAN AND
ENDED IN THE SAME PRISON CELL
ANTONIO BIANCANI (1699-1746)
A BANKER OF MILAN, Italy,
WAS BORN IN A CELL IN THE
STATE PRISON, AND 47 YEARS
LATER, AFTER HIS CONVICTION
FOR HIGH TREASON
*WENT TO HIS DEATH
FROM THE SAME CELL*

THE NEST OF THE GREAT SILVER WATER BEETLE IS BUILT OUT OF 2 CONCAVE LEAVES *AND EQUIPPED WITH A SNORKEL* - TO SUPPLY AIR TO THE BEETLE'S LARVA

McKINLEY ROCK A STONE PROFILE NEAR Thurmond, W.Va., WAS CREATED WHILE BLASTING FOR A RAILROAD ON Sept. 6, 1901 - *THE DAY ON WHICH PRESIDENT McKINLEY WAS FATALLY SHOT BY AN ASSASSIN*

NANCY JANE CLARK (1844-1947) of Farmington, Kentucky, SAW 9 OF HER GREAT-GRANDSONS GO OVERSEAS TO FIGHT *IN WORLD WAR II*

THE TOWN of DUIRAT
In Southern Tunisia
IS ENTIRELY LOCATED
INSIDE A SINGLE MOUNTAIN

A SIEGE TOWER

CONSTRUCTED FOR JULIUS CAESAR
BY GENERAL TREBONIUS OUTSIDE
THE WALLED CITY OF MARSEILLES
WAS STARTED BY BUILDING A
ROOF OF ANIMAL FUR AND ROPE
TO PROTECT THE WORKMEN
AGAINST THE DEFENDERS' ARROWS
- AND THEN THE ROOF WAS
RAISED HIGHER AND HIGHER
TO A HEIGHT OF 6 STORIES

THE LEAPING SHELL
THE AUSTRALIAN TRIGONIA,
a type of mollusk,
CAN LEAP 14 INCHES

A CHRISTMAS TREE
ERECTED FOR A HOLIDAY
CELEBRATION BY STUDENTS
at Kansas State University
*WAS MADE FROM 2
HUGE TUMBLEWEEDS*

DAVID POLK
A LETTER CARRIER,
of Montrose, Scotland,
TO SAVE THE SOLES
OF HIS BOOTS ALWAYS
WALKED ON TIPTOE

THE
GREAT CASTLE of HIROSAKI
in Japan
HAS STOOD FOR MORE THAN 300 YEARS
- YET ITS FOUNDATION CONSISTS
ONLY OF A PILE OF LOOSE
STONES WITHOUT MORTAR

THE CHATEAU THAT ACTUALLY WAS SOLD FOR PEANUTS

BONAGUIL CASTLE
France

WAS BOUGHT IN 1800
BY JEAN LA GRAVE
FOR 41 BAGS OF PEANUTS!

YAKCOWS of Mongolia
OFFSPRING OF A YAK AND A COW

THE **LEAF BUG** of So. America
AS A DISGUISE
AGAINST ITS
ENEMIES HAS
*HIND LEGS WITH
"CALVES" SHAPED LIKE LEAVES*

GUATEMALA
HAS ITS HIGHLANDS SEPARATED
FROM ITS LOWLANDS BY
*A CHAIN OF 32
ACTIVE VOLCANOES*

A **MONKEY**
OWNED
BY BRITISH
EXPLORER
RICHARD
BURTON
(1821-1890)

*WORE
EARRINGS
WITH REAL
ORIENTAL
PEARLS*

THE **CHORTEN**
OF **TASSIDING, India,**
IS CONSIDERED SO SACRED
*THAT THE MERE SIGHT OF IT
CLEANSES A MAN OF ALL SIN*

102

The **ELECTRIC CHAIR PLANT** (Dionea muscipula) *ELECTROCUTES ITS INSECT VICTIMS*

The **PAGODA of PAIT'ATZE** in Mongolia *WHICH IS 325 FEET HIGH STILL STANDS AND ITS 680 BELLS STILL RING -YET EVERY OTHER STRUCTURE IN THE 900-YEAR-OLD CITY WAS DESTROYED BY A STORM*

○ **Mrs. Kate A. GOULD** of Glencoe, Minn., STILL WORKED AS CASHIER IN THE BOX OFFICE OF A MOVIE THEATRE *AT THE AGE OF 93*

A **COAL MINE**
near Neunkirchen, Saar, Germany,
LOCATED ABOVE THE GROUND

THE **LAUGH** THAT SAVED A LIFE!

LORD NORBURY
(1745-1831)
Chief Justice of Ireland,
GIVEN ONLY A FEW HOURS TO LIVE
SENT WORD TO A DYING FRIEND
"IT WILL BE A DEAD HEAT
BETWEEN US!"
*HIS OWN JEST CAUSED LORD NORBURY
TO LAUGH UPROARIOUSLY
AND DOCTORS CREDITED THE JOKE
WITH SAVING HIS LIFE*

THE **V** FALLS
of Leura, New So. Wales
—FORMED BY THE CONVERGING OF
2 GREAT STREAMS OF WATER

104

THE **DOORWAY** TO **HAPPINESS**

THE GATEWAY of the PAGODA of URGA, Mongolia, WAS USED BY EVERY MONGOLIAN ABOUT TO START ON A JOURNEY, FOR A PERIOD OF 1,000 YEARS

-IN THE BELIEF IT ASSURED TRAVELERS A JOYFUL TRIP

ROGER ZUBARIK
of Goldsboro, N.C.,
PLAYING FOOTBALL WITH THE
Little League Green Bay Packers
SCORED 2 TOUCHDOWNS IN THE FIRST 26 SECONDS OF A GAME (Dec. 8, 1962)

THE **HORN** OF **PLENTY**

A SHELL FOUND IN THE FAR EAST *IS USED AS A CANDY CONTAINER*

THE **LEAF** OF THE UMBRELLA TREE *IS SHAPED LIKE A ROUND FAN*

Dr. Thomas SPENCER
(1679-1754)
THE FIRST WHITE CHILD BORN
in East Greenwich, R.I.,
NEVER STUDIED MEDICINE, BUT WAS
ACCREDITED AS THE COMMUNITY'S
FIRST PHYSICIAN - *MERELY BECAUSE HE WAS HIS PARENTS' 7th SON* -
HE WAS A DOCTOR FOR MORE THAN 50 YEARS

GENERAL GEORGE H. WARD
(1826-1863) of Worcester, Mass.,
WHO LOST A LEG IN THE BATTLE OF
BALLS BLUFF, WAS KILLED AT GETTYSBURG
WHILE LEADING HIS TROOPS
ON A WOODEN LEG AND A CRUTCH
July 3, 1863

CLOCK MADE FOR
KING CHARLES II
FROM A
HUMAN SKULL

106

EDMUND WISEMAN
(1562-1644)
WHOSE FAILURE TO DELIVER A PLEA OF CLEMENCY TO QUEEN ELIZABETH I WAS RESPONSIBLE FOR THE DEATH OF THE EARL OF ESSEX **VOWED HE WOULD NEVER AGAIN SLEEP IN A BED** *HE SLUMBERED IN A TREE WITHOUT BEDDING EVERY NIGHT FOR 43 YEARS* -UNTIL HIS DEATH AT THE AGE OF 82

THE **DEVIL'S TABLE**
Viechtach, Germany
NATURAL STONE FORMATION

MOSQUITOES
PREFER BLONDES— A BRUNETTE'S SKIN OFFERS MORE RESISTANCE

A RACE HORSE in England WAS NAMED:
"CRYTOCHONCHOPAYASTIGMATIC"

KING KUMARA DASA

who ruled Ceylon from 515 to 524 WAS SO FERVENT AN ADMIRER OF THE WORKS OF HIS COURT POET, KALIDASA, THAT HE *KILLED HIMSELF BY LEAPING ONTO THE POET'S FUNERAL PYRE*

JOSÉ LUIS

of La Roda, Spain, — WAS STRICKEN WITH PNEUMONIA **32** TIMES *-AND EACH TIME RECOVERED WITHOUT THE USE OF PENICILLIN*

THE GUARDIAN OF THE NOTCH

A HUNTER AND HIS DOG *NATURAL STONE FORMATION* Smugglers Notch, Cambridge, Vt.

BAMBOO MONEY
USED IN THE
19TH CENTURY BY
THE CHINESE

KING EDWARD IV
(1442-1482) of England
*WAS THE FIRST ROYAL
FISHERMAN IN HISTORY*
KING EDWARD, WHO ADOPTED
THE SPORT FORMERLY ENGAGED
IN ONLY BY HIS MOST HUMBLE
SUBJECTS, CAUGHT A FATAL
COLD WHILE FISHING

EPIPHYTIC
ORCHIDS
GROW IN THE
BRANCHES OF
HIGH TREES AND
**EACH HAS 3
TYPES OF ROOTS**
ONE TYPE OF
ROOT SUPPORTS
THE ORCHID BY
TWINING AROUND
BRANCHES,
ANOTHER DROPS
TO THE GROUND
TO DRAW
NOURISHMENT FROM
THE SOIL, AND THE
THIRD TYPE ABSORBS
MOISTURE FROM THE AIR

A **COIN**
MINTED IN
Korea in 1464
WAS SHAPED
LIKE AN ARROWHEAD
4 INCHES IN LENGTH

THE **MEMORIAL** in Dartmouth, England, TO THE DEAD OF WORLD WARS I AND II *ORIGINALLY SERVED AS A BAPTISMAL FONT* **300 YEARS AGO**

DROPS OF BLOOD FROM THE FINGER OF MACHINIST MATTHEW MATHIS, BLOTTED UP BY A PIECE OF COPY PAPER, FORMED A PERFECT PICTURE *OF A FRENCH POODLE*

Submitted by DOROTHY HAMILL Johnson City, Tenn.

JAMES FLETCHER of Terryville, Conn., IS THE WINNER OF **11 MEDALS** and **13 TROPHIES** FOR ROLLER SKATING, AND WAS *THE* MEN'S FIGURE-SKATING CHAMPION OF CONNECTICUT. *-YET HE HAS A PARALYZED LEG, AND SKATES WITH METAL BRACES*

110

CAVE FISH of Mexico ARE SIGHTLESS – YET THEY HAVE SUCH SENSITIVE "RADAR" *THEY NEVER COLLIDE WITH ANYTHING*

JOHN ERICSSON
(1803–1889)
The famed naval engineer

WAS OFFICIAL DRAFTSMAN OF THE SWEDISH CANAL COMPANY **AT THE AGE OF 12**

HE HEADED A LABOR FORCE OF 400 MEN IN THE CONSTRUCTION OF SWEDEN'S GÖTA CANAL WHEN HE WAS ONLY 14

THE **FIRST TOOL**

A STONE AXE found at St. Acheul, France WAS CARVED BEFORE THE AGE OF MAN *1,000,000 YEARS AGO*

THE **OLDEST TAVERN IN THE U.S.**
THE WHITE HOUSE TAVERN in Newport, R.I., *HAS BEEN OPERATING FOR 291 YEARS*

4 AUSTRIAN OFFICIALS

WHO REGULARLY ROWED TOGETHER EACH SUNDAY ON THE DANUBE

WERE ORDERED DROWNED BY PRINCE VON KAUNITZ, CHANCELLOR OF AUSTRIA, *BECAUSE HE HAD LEARNED ONE OF THEM WAS A SPY FOR PRUSSIA*

-YET THE PRINCE KNEW THE OTHER 3 MEN WERE INNOCENT

PENNIES in British West Africa in 1936 *WERE MADE OF **NICKEL***

THE ROCK IGUANA

GUANA ISLAND, in the Virgin Is. *NATURAL STONE FORMATION*

THE HUGE THRONE OF King Mpande of the Zulus **WAS CARVED FROM A SINGLE BLOCK OF WOOD**

NATIVES of the Quiquijana Tribe of Cuzco, Peru, **IN A DANCE IMPERSONATING A STORM-TOSSED SHIP—MUST BALANCE A MAST 20 FEET HIGH**

STONE HEAD Submitted by ERIC LEVY Revere, Mass.

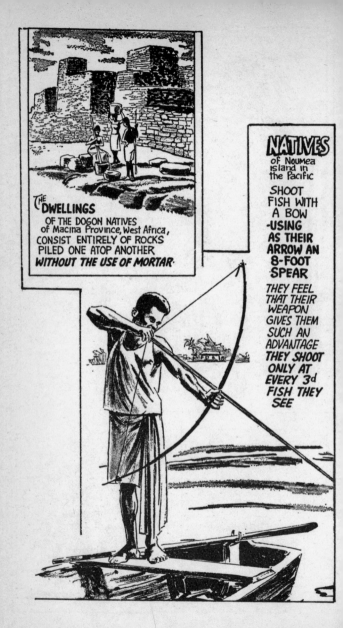

THE DWELLINGS
OF THE DOGON NATIVES of Macina Province, West Africa, CONSIST ENTIRELY OF ROCKS PILED ONE ATOP ANOTHER *WITHOUT THE USE OF MORTAR*

NATIVES of Noumea island in the Pacific

SHOOT FISH WITH A BOW -USING AS THEIR ARROW AN 8-FOOT SPEAR

THEY FEEL THAT THEIR WEAPON GIVES THEM SUCH AN ADVANTAGE THEY SHOOT ONLY AT EVERY 3d FISH THEY SEE

IF A YOUNG TWIN DIES IN THE YORUBA TRIBE of Nigeria, Africa, THE SURVIVOR MUST CARRY AROUND A WOODEN STATUE OF THE DEAD TWIN -WHICH IS CLOTHED LIKE THE SURVIVING TWIN EVERY DAY AND GIVEN THE SAME FOOD

THE TEMPLE ON THE THRONE OF SOLOMON a mountain near Srinagar, Kashmir, WAS BUILT IN 220 B.C. OF LOOSE STONES WITHOUT MORTAR -YET IT HAS ENDURED FOR NEARLY 22 CENTURIES

THE **CITY** of **DUNFERMLINE** in Scotland

WAS LEASED TO QUEEN ANNE BY HER HUSBAND, KING JAMES VI, **FOR THE ANNUAL RENTAL OF ONE PENNY**

THE PENNY WAS PAYABLE EACH YEAR ON THE 7th SUNDAY AFTER EASTER - AND IF THE QUEEN HAD FAILED TO MAKE A SINGLE PAYMENT ON TIME THE CITY WOULD HAVE REVERTED TO THE KING

SHE WAS
TWICE 6
TWICE 7
TWICE 20
AND 11

INSCRIPTION ON TOMBSTONE Churchyard of Wistanstow, England

DR. CHARLES STEINMETZ the electrical wizard

NEVER LEARNED TO OPERATE A CAR *BECAUSE HE HIT A TREE ON HIS FIRST ATTEMPT TO DRIVE*

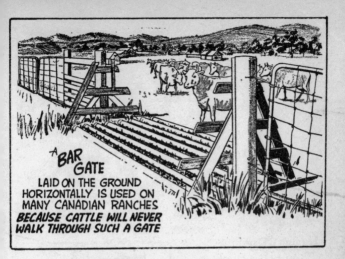

A BAR GATE
LAID ON THE GROUND HORIZONTALLY IS USED ON MANY CANADIAN RANCHES *BECAUSE CATTLE WILL NEVER WALK THROUGH SUCH A GATE*

MOHAMMED IQBAL (1876-1938)
AN INDIAN POET IN HIS EPIC POEMS
FIRST SUGGESTED THE CREATION OF THE INDEPENDENT MOHAMMEDAN STATE OF PAKISTAN

General Postage.
NOT EXCEEDING HALF AN OUNCE.
One Penny.

A POSTAGE STAMP
WAS SUGGESTED TO THE BRITISH GOVERNMENT BY JAMES CHALMERS, of Dundee, in 1834
-6 YEARS BEFORE OFFICIAL INVENTION OF THE POSTAGE STAMP BY ROWLAND HILL

COLOGNE, Germany,

FOR DEMOLISHING ITS 700-YEAR-OLD CITY WALLS WITHOUT FIRST GETTING APPROVAL OF THE PRUSSIAN GOVERNMENT, WAS ORDERED TO WEIGH THE DEBRIS AND PAY THE GOVERNMENT *ITS "ASSESSED VALUE" OF $3,000,000* (1881)

THE **FAT-RUMPED SHEEP** of Asia and Africa ARE PROTECTED AGAINST PERIODS OF FAMINE *BY A LAYER OF FAT STORED ON THEIR BACKS*

THE **TOMBS** of Haitian peasants ARE OFTEN RESPLENDENT STRUCTURES *EVEN THOUGH THEY MAY HAVE LIVED ALL THEIR LIVES IN WRETCHED HUTS*

THE MARBLE STATUE
of Lady Jane Cheyne
in Chelsea Old Church, London, England,
WAS BLOWN THROUGH A SOLID
STONE WALL BY A NAZI BOMB IN
WORLD WAR II AND BURIED IN
THE RUBBLE OF THE CHURCH
• *YET IT WAS FOUND UNDAMAGED
EXCEPT FOR MINOR SCRATCHES*

THE **TOMB OF CYRUS THE GREAT**
FOUNDER OF THE PERSIAN EMPIRE
located in Pasargadae, Iran,
HAS BEEN THE RESIDENCE OF A
SUCCESSION OF FORTUNE TELLERS
FOR 2,000 YEARS

THE **GOBLIN** of
Narvik,
Norway

NATURAL
STONE
FORMATION

School Children in Chad, Africa, TO SHOW THEIR RESPECT *TURN THEIR BACKS TO THEIR TEACHERS*

A GREAT WINDOW in the Manor of Leybourne, England, *SERVES AS A SUN DIAL*

SIGN IN WEST FALMOUTH, MASS.

A HUGE BOULDER near Arequipa, Peru, SPLIT OPEN BY A CACTUS

A WOMAN of the Motilones Tribe of Colombia DANCING IN TRIBAL FESTIVITIES MUST CARRY ON HER BACK *A BAG FILLED WITH THE BONES OF DECEASED RELATIVES*

THE STABLES BUILT IN SAAS-FEE, Switzerland, ARE ALWAYS REPLICAS OF THE DWELLINGS CONSTRUCTED BY THE TOWN'S ANCESTORS *IN ANCIENT TIMES*

LONGLEAT HOUSE
in England
WAS RENOVATED IN 1808 BY
THE 2d MARQUESS OF BATH
WHO RAISED THE FUNDS BY
COLLECTING FROM EACH
TENANT ON HIS ESTATE
20 YEARS' RENT IN ADVANCE

RALPH SIEDEL
of Strongsville, Ohio,
A GRADUATE OF
WILMINGTON COLLEGE,
WORE A CAP AND
GOWN PURCHASED BY
HIS FAMILY IN 1927
*AND WORN BY 28
MEMBERS OF THE
FAMILY AND FRIENDS*

THE OLDEST WIG IN THE WORLD
IT WAS FOUND IN
THE GRAVE OF
EGYPTIAN PRINCESS
ENTIU-NY AND
WAS INTERRED
WITH HER IN
1049 B.C.

*—MORE THAN
3,000
YEARS AGO*

Timothy
McCARY
of Birmingham,
Alabama,
AT ONE YEAR
OF AGE
HAD 13
LIVING
GRANDPARENTS

THE COWBOY BAND
of Dodge City, Kansas,
WAS LED FROM 1881 TO 1887
BY A BANDLEADER
WHO USED AS HIS BATON A
LOADED SIX-SHOOTER

PROFILE ROCK
near Gehlberg, Germany,
ACTUALLY HAS 2 PROFILES
CARVED BY NATURE
-ON ONE SIDE THAT OF A MAN, AND
ON THE OTHER THE HEAD OF A DOG

LEMON
SHAPED LIKE THE
HEAD OF A WITCH
found by Susie and
Donna Hardwick
Los Angeles, Calif.

The
STATUES that
**CHANGED THEIR
COIFFURES**
**EMPRESS ANNA
LUCILLA** (147-183)
of Rome
HAD A NUMBER
OF WIGS OF
VARIOUS HUES
—SO EVERY
STATUE OF THE
EMPRESS WAS
CREATED WITH
**INTERCHANGEABLE
MARBLE
HAIRDOS**

PUMPKINS, GROWING IN Um Ramad, Sudan,
ON THE THATCHED ROOF OF A HOUSE

A PUBLIC LIBRARY
WAS ESTABLISHED IN Chicago, Illinois, in 1871 *IN AN ABANDONED WATER TANK*

A **TOMATO PLANT** GROWING OUT OF A CONCRETE YARD in Sydney, Australia, HAS REACHED A HEIGHT OF **19** FEET - *AND IS STILL GROWING*

Submitted by Edward O'Sullivan Fairfield. New So. Wales

GENERAL NORD-ALEXIS (1820-1910) STARTED THE REVOLUTION WHICH OVERTHREW THE GOVERNMENT OF HAITI IN 1902 *WHEN HE WAS 82 YEARS OF AGE*

A **CASH** REGISTER
USED EVERY
WEEKDAY
*FOR 53
YEARS*

Submitted by
Allen Munro
Malden, Mass.

HENRY CAREY

OVER A PERIOD OF 80 YEARS
**WAS VALET TO 6
BRITISH RULERS**

*HE SERVED JAMES I, CHARLES I,
OLIVER CROMWELL, CHARLES II,
JAMES II AND WILLIAM III*
(1615 - 1695)

Gladiolus
WITH 4
FLOWERING
STEMS

Submitted by
MRS. ALICE FEILING
Kentfield, Calif.

ANTS
TO CROSS
FROM ONE LEAF
TO ANOTHER
FORM A LIVING BRIDGE

YOUNG LAMBS
BECAUSE OF A SHORTAGE OF SHEEP DOGS in Syria *ARE TRAINED TO GUARD THE FLOCKS*

THE **STONE CAMEL**
NATURAL FORMATION
Luray Caverns, Virginia

ANDREW MILLS of Spennymoor, England, HANGED AND PLACED IN A CAGE FOR THE MURDER OF 3 CHILDREN, *REMAINED ALIVE ON THE SCAFFOLD FOR SEVERAL DAYS*

THE **COEDARHYDYGLYN HOUSE**
atop Tumble Hill, in Glamorgan, Wales,
**OVERLOOKS 7 COUNTIES
IN WALES AND ENGLAND**

THE FLOWER THAT "WALKS"
NEOMATICA GRACIALIS
a form of Iris
*BENDS OVER UNTIL ITS BLOOM
TOUCHES THE GROUND
- AND THEN TAKES ROOT A STEP
AWAY FROM THE MOTHER PLANT*

*VALMONT
SONIAT* DUFOSSAT
WHO WAS A PLANTER IN
NEW ORLEANS IN THE 1840's
*IS REMEMBERED IN THAT
CITY BY STREETS BEARING
EACH OF HIS 3 NAMES*

128

THE LANTERN COFFEE POT

USED IN ENGLAND IN 1692 HAD GLASS INSETS SO THAT WHEN IT WAS NOT BEING USED TO BREW COFFEE *IT COULD SERVE AS A LANTERN*

ROBERT E. CRADDOCK

of Warren County, Ky., A VETERAN OF THE AMERICAN REVOLUTION AROSE FROM HIS DEATHBED UNASSISTED, DONNED HIS UNIFORM AND HAD A PIPER AND DRUMMER MARCH AROUND HIS HOME

-SO HE COULD ENJOY HIS OLD REGIMENTAL MARCHES AS THE LAST SOUNDS HE WOULD HEAR ON EARTH (1837)

SHETLAND ISLAND SHEEP

ARE NOT SHORN *THEIR WOOL IS PLUCKED OUT*

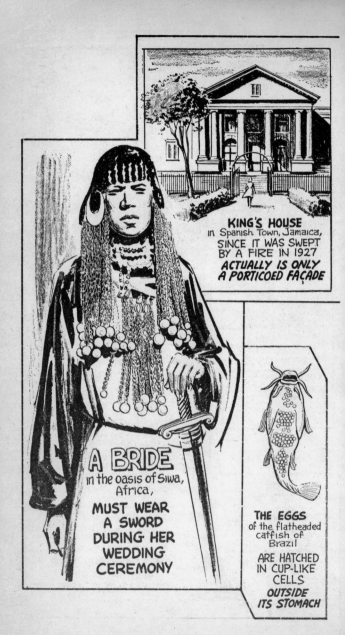

KING'S HOUSE in Spanish Town, Jamaica, SINCE IT WAS SWEPT BY A FIRE IN 1927 *ACTUALLY IS ONLY A PORTICOED FAÇADE*

A BRIDE in the oasis of Siwa, Africa, **MUST WEAR A SWORD DURING HER WEDDING CEREMONY**

THE EGGS of the flatheaded catfish of Brazil **ARE HATCHED IN CUP-LIKE CELLS** *OUTSIDE ITS STOMACH*

"VOS OMNES"
AN ANCIENT ROMAN EXPRESSION MEANING **"YOU ALL"**

JOHN MYTTON
(1796 - 1834)
of Halston, England,
CURED HIMSELF OF
HICCOUGHING
**BY SETTING FIRE
TO HIS NIGHTSHIRT!**
*HE HAD A NARROW
ESCAPE FROM DEATH - BUT
IT CURED HIS HICCOUGHS*

THE **SIMPLEST CENSUS IN HISTORY**
Persia, KNOWING THAT EACH OF ITS CITIZENS
CONSUMED ONE LOAF OF BREAD A DAY,
*FOR CENTURIES ESTIMATED ITS POPULATION
MERELY BY* **COUNTING THE NUMBER
OF LOAVES SOLD IN THE COUNTRY**

THE **IRON** CLUB
WEIGHING **2** POUNDS
WITH WHICH
APPRENTICES WERE
CHASTISED IN THE
LABOR GUILDS
OF EUROPE
*WAS OFFICIALLY
CERTIFIED —AND
CALLED "JUSTICE"*

KATHERYN TUDOR
(1535-1591) of Berain, Wales,
ACCEPTED **2** PROPOSALS OF
MARRIAGE IN 1566 DURING THE
FUNERAL OF HER 1st HUSBAND

MAURICE WYNNE BECAME HER **2nd**
HUSBAND AND WHEN HE DIED IN
1570 SHE MARRIED SIR RICHARD
CLOUGH—HAVING ASSURED HIM AT
THE GRAVE OF HER FIRST HUSBAND
**THAT SHE WOULD MARRY
HIM AFTER THE DEATH OF
HER SECOND SPOUSE !**
*SHE ALSO BURIED SIR RICHARD
AND IN 1580 TOOK EDWARD
THELWALL AS HER 4th HUSBAND*

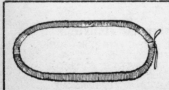

AN **ORNAMENTAL BELT**
WORN BY SHILLUK TRIBESMEN
of the White Nile, in Africa,
*CONSISTS OF THIN
DISKS MADE FROM
THE SHELLS OF
OSTRICH EGGS*

JUSTICE PHILIP J. McCOOK of New York WAS A CORPORAL IN THE SPANISH-AMERICAN WAR, A MAJOR IN WORLD WAR I *AND WAS MADE A COLONEL IN WORLD WAR II AT THE AGE OF 69*

THE **MARKET** of Antigua, Guatemala, IS LOCATED IN THE RUINS OF AN OLD CHURCH

NEPHILA MACULATA A GIANT SPIDER OF INDIA, EXUDES AN OIL FROM ITS SALIVARY GLANDS *TO KEEP FROM GETTING STUCK IN ITS OWN WEB*

OYSTER SHELLS ARE USED IN THE WEST CAROLINE ISLANDS IN THE PACIFIC *AS MONEY*

FOOTMEN
AT THE ROYAL CASTLE of Amalienborg, Denmark, WEAR AS PART OF THEIR ORNATE HEADGEAR *POTS FILLED WITH ARTIFICIAL FLOWERS*

ROBERT QUIRKE, KEEPING A VOW MADE WHEN HIS SHIP WAS IN DANGER OF FOUNDERING IN THE BAY OF BISCAY, SCRAPPED THE VESSEL ON HIS SAFE RETURN TO MINEHEAD, ENGLAND, AND USED ITS LUMBER TO BUILD *11 ALMSHOUSES* –WHICH ARE STILL STANDING 333 YEARS LATER

"DACHSHUND" SHEEP DEVELOPED BY A BREEDER In Oslo, Norway, *HAVE SHORT LEGS AND LONG BODIES*

STEVE McCANN
of Eau Claire, Wis.,
WHO ENLISTED IN THE UNION
ARMY DURING THE CIVIL WAR
*SERVED IN THE 1ST
WISCONSIN REGIMENT*
WITH 7 OF HIS SONS
AND 2 SONS-IN-LAW

**SEWARD V.
COFFIN**
(1867 - 1948)
of Middletown, Conn.,
VACATIONED AT THE
SAME HOTEL AT
BLUE MOUNTAIN
LAKE, NEW YORK,
*EVERY SUMMER
FOR 70
YEARS*

A BARREL OF WINE WAS ROLLED BY
2 GERMANS NAMED PUETZ AND MAINZER
FROM BERNKASTEL TO BERLIN
– A DISTANCE OF 500 MILES

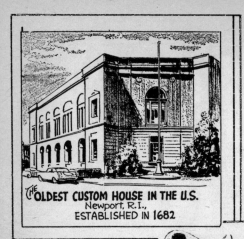

THE OLDEST CUSTOM HOUSE IN THE U.S.
Newport, R.I.,
ESTABLISHED IN 1682

THE "FLICKER FISH" of Tahiti
ARE BANDED BLACK AND WHITE — A CAMOUFLAGE THAT MAKES THEM APPEAR TO BE JUST *A FLICKER OF LIGHT AND SHADOW ON THE WATER*

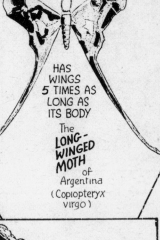

HAS WINGS 5 TIMES AS LONG AS ITS BODY

The LONG-WINGED MOTH of Argentina
(Copiopteryx virgo)

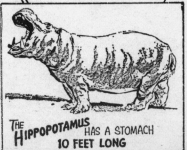

THE HIPPOPOTAMUS HAS A STOMACH 10 FEET LONG

136

THE STONE OWL
NATURAL ROCK FORMATION
Blue Mountains of Jamaica

THE LADY GUARDIAN OF THE RAVINE OF DALUIS
France
NATURAL STONE FORMATION

THE **LEAD** ROOF
of Temple Church,
in London, England,
MELTING IN A FIRE
DURING THE LONDON
BLITZ ON MAY 10, 1941,
FLOWED TO THE FLOOR
OF THE SANCTUARY
AND THEN COOLED
IN THE SHAPE OF
THE BRITISH LION
—*EMBLEM OF THE
NATION'S SPIRIT
OF DEFIANCE*

THE "**Y**" **BRIDGE**
Lyons Falls, N.Y.

BASKETS
ARE WOVEN
FROM THE
**BURITI
PALM**
BY THE
**BAKAIRI
INDIANS**
of Brazil
*IN LESS
THAN 10
MINUTES*

POTATO VALENTINE
Submitted by BYRON TRASTER
Fairmount, Ind.

THE JAIL in Niagara Falls, Canada, BUILT IN 1817, HAD CELLS WITH NO WINDOWS AND NO HEAT FOR CRIMINALS, *BUT THOSE FOR DEBTORS HAD BOTH WINDOWS AND FIREPLACES*

SPIES IN THE MEXICAN WAR OF 1847-48 WERE INSTANTLY IDENTIFIABLE *BECAUSE THEY WORE A PRESCRIBED MILITARY UNIFORM*

THE **PARCHMENT WORM** BUILDS A U-SHAPED TUBE AT THE BOTTOM OF THE SEA, THEN PUMPS WATER THROUGH THIS NEST *SO IT CAN FEED UPON THE MICROSCOPIC CREATURES OF THE SEA*

A **TURNIP** IN THE SHAPE OF A SHRIVELED HAND IS REGARDED BY GERMAN FARMERS AS A SIGN THAT THEY WILL HAVE POOR CROPS

Alexander THE **GREAT** *HAD ONE BLACK EYE AND ONE BLUE EYE*

DANIEL DURBIN of Seattle, Wash., HIS MOTHER, MRS. MARGARET BROWN DURBIN, AND HIS GRANDFATHER, HAROLD BROWN, *ALL WERE BORN ON JULY 12TH*

A WASHING MACHINE SOLD IN THE U.S. IN THE 1800's, WAS MOUNTED ON ROCKING-CHAIR LEGS SO THE CLOTHING *COULD BE ROCKED CLEAN*

HERMAN MARCUS of Vicksburg, Miss., PLAYING GOLF AT THE VICKSBURG COUNTRY CLUB IN 1937, SHOT A HOLE-IN-ONE ON THE SECOND HOLE

-AND SCORED ANOTHER HOLE-IN-ONE 25 YEARS LATER ON THE SAME HOLE

HENRY CAVENDISH (1731-1810) THE ENGLISH CHEMIST AND PHYSICIST, WAS SO SHY IN THE PRESENCE OF WOMEN THAT HE BUILT A SEPARATE STAIRCASE IN HIS HOME *THAT THE HOUSEMAIDS WERE FORBIDDEN TO USE*

LEATHER WINE BOTTLES in medieval times *WERE SHAPED LIKE THE ANIMALS FROM WHOSE PELTS THE BOTTLES WERE MADE*

ARTHUR RIMBAUD (1854-1891) CELEBRATED FRENCH POET, ENTERED COLLEGE AT *THE AGE OF 10*

THE SHIVA TEMPLE
of Utterkashi, India,
WAS BUILT TO ENSHRINE AN
ANCIENT PILLAR OF METAL
26 FEET HIGH
BECAUSE IT HAS MYSTERIOUSL
REMAINED FREE OF RUST
FOR 2,400 YEARS

CAN A
MAGNET
PICK UP
A U.S.
COIN?
(Answer
tomorrow)

ROCK
WITH A
PERFECT
OUTLINE
OF THE
NUMBER 1
Submitted by
MIKE THOMPSON,
Glendive,
Montana

Emperor **ALEXANDER I**
of Russia
ONCE SUFFERED A HEADACHE
THAT COST **$10,000,000** !

THE COURT DOCTOR ORDERED CANDLES SO
THE EMPEROR COULD INHALE THEIR SMOKE--
BUT **91** YEARS LATER **4,000,000** TAPERS
WERE FOUND IN THE PALACE--BECAUSE NO
ONE HAD CANCELLED THE **DAILY DELIVERY**
OF CANDLES !

141

Cardinal
THOMAS WOLSEY (1475-1530)
LORD CHANCELLOR of ENGLAND,
WHILE ATTENDING
THE HOUSE OF LORDS
*ALWAYS BROUGHT ALONG
HIS FAVORITE CAT*

THE **TOWER** of the Church of Foulden, England,
COLLAPSED MORE THAN 200 YEARS AGO,
BUT THE DEBRIS HAS NEVER BEEN CLEARED AWAY IN THE
HOPE IT MAY SOMEDAY BE USED IN REBUILDING THE SPIRE

THE MEMORIALS TO 8 MISTAKES!

Gumbum, Mongolia,

8 LAMAS TRICKED INTO ATTENDING A CONFERENCE WITH A CHINESE GENERAL, WERE EACH ASKED IF HE COULD PREDICT **THE DAY ON WHICH HE WOULD DIE**

THE FRIGHTENED LAMAS ALL REPLIED "TOMORROW," BUT THEY WERE BEHEADED THAT VERY DAY

—AND 8 WHITE TOWERS NOW STAND ON THE SITE OF THEIR EXECUTION TO COMMEMORATE THEIR ERROR

THE TOWER of the Parish Church in Ashwell, England, BUILT BY THOMAS EVERARD 248 YEARS AGO, CARRIES ON ITS ROOF THIS INSCRIPTION:

"Thomas Everard placed me here, He said to last a hundred year"

GRAPE VINES ON ROANOKE ISLAND, N.C., *ARE MORE THAN* **300 YEARS OLD**

3 WHITE COWS
ARE GIVEN ANNUALLY BY THE
SHEPHERDS of Baratous, France,
TO THOSE of Roncal, Spain,
AS PAYMENT TO THE
SPANISH SHEPHERDS FOR
HAVING PERMITTED BARATOUS
TO BECOME PART OF FRANCE
587 YEARS AGO

THE **COUNT de CUSTINE**
of France,
WHO BECAME FAMOUS AS
"GENERAL MUSTACHE" WHILE
SERVING IN THE AMERICAN
REVOLUTION, HAD ENTERED THE
FRENCH ARMY AS A LIEUTENANT
AT THE AGE OF 7

THE **FIRST MAIL-ORDER HOUSE**
A ONE-ROOM HOUSE,
PREFABRICATED IN CHICAGO, ILL.,
WAS ADVERTISED IN AN 1870
CATALOGUE FOR **$175**

THE
**GIANT
CRAB-EATING
FROG**
SWALLOWS
CRABS IN
THEIR SHELLS

THE **TEMPLE of HEAVEN** in Peking, China, INCLUDED AN ALTAR SO SACRED THAT FOR *CENTURIES ONLY THE CHINESE EMPEROR COULD STAND ON IT*

THE **BIRTHPLACE** of the **TELEPHONE** ALEXANDER GRAHAM BELL CONDUCTED HIS EXPERIMENTS ON THE TOP FLOOR OF THE BUILDING AT 109 COURT ST., IN BOSTON, MASS., AND *IN 1875 FIRST SUC-CEEDED IN TRANSMITTING SPEECH BY ELECTRICITY*

THE **BATHS** at Tambo Machay, Peru, BUILT OF GRANITE BLOCKS BY THE INCAS, WAS CONSTRUCTED WITHOUT MORTAR, YET THE ROCKS FIT SO TIGHTLY THAT A KNIFE BLADE CAN-NOT BE **INSERTED BETWEEN THEM**

The **Earl of Angus** (1489-1557) AS A BOY FELL IN LOVE WITH QUEEN MARGARET of Scotland, SISTER OF KING HENRY VIII, **AND WHEN HE GREW UP MARRIED 3 MARGARETS IN SUCCESSION** -HIS SECOND WIFE BEING QUEEN MARGARET HERSELF, WHO HAD BECOME A WIDOW IN 1513

THE **GOLDEN DOMES OF KADIMAIN** Bagdad THE CUPOLAS OF THIS MOSQUE ARE COVERED WITH SHEETS OF **SOLID GOLD ONE INCH THICK AND VALUED AT $1,300,000!**

A LOG CABIN ON TILICUM ISLAND, PA., BUILT BY SWEDISH SETTLERS IN 1650, *IS STILL USABLE 326 YEARS LATER*

THE
10TH EARL
OF
DUNDONALD
1775-1860
A BRITISH ADMIRAL,
CREATED A SECRET WEAPON WHICH SO
HORRIFIED THE ADMIRALTY THAT
**HIS INVENTION WAS ORDERED
SEALED FROM VIEW FOREVER**

*55 YEARS AFTER THE ADMIRAL'S DEATH
WINSTON CHURCHILL BROKE THE SEAL AND
LEARNED THE INVENTION WAS POISON GAS*
**- BUT THE GERMANS WERE
ALREADY USING IT**

A **HINDU PAGODA** in Madura, India,
THAT IS TOPPED BY A CHRISTIAN CROSS
IT I'S ONE OF 17 SUCH CHURCHES IN INDIA THAT SERVE THE
ASHRAM BROTHERHOOD, A HINDU CHRISTIAN SECT

147

IRON BELLS CARRIED IN THE AFRICAN CONGO BY THE FOLLOWERS OF A NATIVE PRINCE AS THE SYMBOL OF HIS AUTHORITY

JOSEPH STALIN (1879-1953) THE SOVIET RULER, TO RAISE MONEY FOR THE MARXIST CAUSE, AS A YOUTH, *WAS A BANK ROBBER*

THE **MONKEY-EATING EAGLE** WHICH FEEDS ON MONKEYS AND LARGE BIRDS, *IS FOUND ONLY IN THE PHILIPPINES*

148

THE GROUND CUCKOO
*CAN RUN AS FAST AS
A RACEHORSE*

ELEVATORS
IN DEPARTMENT STORES
IN THE LATE 1800's WERE
ORNATELY DECORATED
AND FURNISHED
*WITH SEATS FOR
PASSENGERS*

John PARRY
famed 18th-
century harpist,
WAS THE BEST CHECKERS
PLAYER IN ALL WALES
—*YET HE WAS TOTALLY BLIND*

HORSES WERE SOLD
in Australia in 1924
FOR ONE CENT EACH

THE LEAF FISH SWIMMING HEAD DOWN, LOOKS LIKE A DRY, BROWN LEAF DRIFTING IN THE WATER

ELIAS HOWE (1819-1867) of Spencer, Mass., INVENTOR OF THE SEWING MACHINE, HAVING GONE TO ENGLAND IN AN ATTEMPT TO GET FINANCIAL BACKING, BECAME SO IMPOVERISHED THAT TO PAY HIS PASSAGE HOME, **HE PAWNED HIS MODEL AND PATENT PAPERS**

A **MONUMENT** IN KINHASA, THE CONGO, COMMEMORATING THE INTRODUCTION OF THE RAILROAD, DEPICTS *THE HUMAN CARRIERS WHO FORMERLY TRANSPORTED ALL CARGOES*

THE **MOTMOT** of Mexico ALWAYS RIPS BIG GAPS IN ITS TAIL FEATHERS

MRS. **OLIVE WALKER** OF WORPLESDON, SURREY, ENGLAND, A GRANDMOTHER, WAS THE VILLAGE'S **CHIMNEY SWEEP**

THE CASTLE A MAN BUILT TO ESCAPE HIS SHADOW
Puxerloch, Austria
CHARLOT a knight of Charlemagne, CONSTRUCTED A FORTRESS IN A CAVE AND LEFT IT ONLY ON MOONLESS NIGHTS *SO HIS SHADOW COULD NEVER PURSUE HIM*

LEATHERJACKET
*THE FISH THAT CAN'T BE SCALED.
ITS SCALES ARE SET AT
VARIOUS ANGLES*

TABLE ROCK
NATURAL FORMATION THAT STOOD FOR YEARS IN LINCOLN COUNTY, KANSAS

THE **TETHYS** IN A PERIOD OF 4 MONTHS, LAYS **478,000,000 EGGS**

THE **MISTAKE THAT SAVED A CITY!**
*THE MANGIA TOWER, in Siena, Italy,
WAS NAMED FOR ITS FIRST
BELLRINGER, WHO RANG THE
BELLS BY ERROR IN 1348
-AROUSING THE TOWNSPEOPLE
JUST IN TIME TO FIGHT OFF
A MIDNIGHT ATTACK*

THE 'FROZEN' WATERFALL
THE CAVE OF GARGAS, NEAR
Saint-Bertrand-de-Comminges, France
A MASS OF STALACTITES

DANIEL ANTHONY
BROTHER OF
SUSAN B.
ANTHONY, THE
SUFFRAGETTE,
HIMSELF A
CONTROVERSIAL
EDITOR OF THE
LEAVENWORTH,
KANSAS,
"CONSERVATIVE,"
*WAS SHOT AT
5 TIMES,
BEATEN AND
HORSEWHIPPED
AT THE AGE
OF 67*

FRENCHMEN
IN THE
1780'S WORE
THEIR HAIR, OR
WIGS, PATTERNED
*AFTER THE
HEDGEHOG*

THE LARGEST BEEHIVE IN THE WORLD

BEE ROCK NEAR Sublimity Springs, Laurel County, Ky., ONCE HOUSED SO MANY BEES THAT WHEN THEY FLEW AWAY IN SEARCH OF NECTAR *THEY DARKENED THE SKY*

AN **ANCIENT GRAVE MARKER** CARVED BY ROMANS, VISIBLE IN THE WALL OF THE PARISH CHURCH OF HIRSAU, GERMANY

WILLIAM HENRY HARRISON PORTRAYED BY HIS FOLLOWERS AS A PLOW-PUSHING MAN OF THE PEOPLE IN THE U.S. PRESIDENTIAL CAMPAIGN OF 1840-- *ACTUALLY WAS A WEALTHY VIRGINIA PLANTER*

4-LEGGED CHICKEN
Submitted by
MRS. HILTON
TORREYSON,
Tompkinsville, Md.

JOHANN PETER LYSER
(1803-1870) of Germany
WAS CELEBRATED AS A PAINTER,
POET, MUSICIAN AND MUSIC
CRITIC IN DRESDEN, VIENNA
AND BERLIN FOR 33 YEARS
*-YET THROUGHOUT THAT ENTIRE
PERIOD HE WAS TOTALLY* **DEAF**

THE CATHEDRAL OF SAINT-MALO
France
CONDEMNED DURING THE FRENCH
REVOLUTION, WAS SOLD TO A FISHERMAN
ON HIS PLEDGE TO
REDUCE IT TO RUBBLE!
*KNOWING THE CHURCH COULD NOT BE
HARMED WITHOUT ITS OWNER'S SANCTION
-ITS PURCHASER VANISHED AND WAS
NEVER SEEN AGAIN!*

THE STAY-AT-HOME BIRD
THE NIHOE MILLERBIRD
IS FOUND NOWHERE
IN THE WORLD
EXCEPT ON THE
146 ACRES OF
NIHOA, HAWAII

DR. HIPOLITO IRIGOYEN
(1850-1933)
RE-ELECTED PRESIDENT OF ARGENTINA IN 1928, AFTER HAVING BEEN OUT OF OFFICE FOR 6 YEARS, REFUSED TO MOVE INTO THE PRESIDENTIAL PALACE --
LIVING INSTEAD IN AN APARTMENT OVER A STORE

THE ELM TREE GRAVE
Catherine de Bogart of Woodstock, N.Y., DIED AS A RESULT OF A BEATING AND WAS BURIED STILL GRASPING THE ELM TREE SWITCH
-WHICH GREW INTO A HUGE TREE THAT FORCED ITS WAY UP THROUGH HER GRAVESTONE

A FORD RUNABOUT
IN 1923
SOLD FOR $265

The Rev.
Thomas
LINDLEY

WAS
CURATE OF
HALTON GILL,
England,
*FOR 70
YEARS*

DR. ALICE HAMILTON
IN 1919 BECAME THE FIRST WOMAN
ADMITTED TO HARVARD'S FACULTY
*BECAUSE SHE WAS THE ONLY PERSON
IN THE COUNTRY QUALIFIED TO TEACH
HER SUBJECT--INDUSTRIAL MEDICINE*

The Rev. T. J.
ZUMWALT
WAS AN
ITINERANT
PREACHER
IN THE
OZARKS FROM
1860 TO 1927
*--A PERIOD
OF 67
YEARS*

DACHSHUNDS
ARE NOT GERMAN
*THEY WERE
KNOWN IN
EGYPT IN
2,000 B.C.*

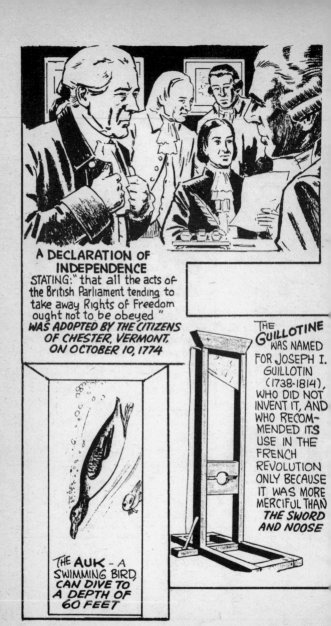

A DECLARATION OF INDEPENDENCE STATING:" that all the acts of the British Parliament tending to take away Rights of Freedom ought not to be obeyed " *WAS ADOPTED BY THE CITIZENS OF CHESTER, VERMONT, ON OCTOBER 10, 1774*

THE GUILLOTINE WAS NAMED FOR JOSEPH I. GUILLOTIN (1738-1814), WHO DID NOT INVENT IT, AND WHO RECOMMENDED ITS USE IN THE FRENCH REVOLUTION ONLY BECAUSE IT WAS MORE MERCIFUL THAN *THE SWORD AND NOOSE*

THE AUK - A SWIMMING BIRD, *CAN DIVE TO A DEPTH OF 60 FEET*

EDWARD PREBLE (1761-1807) AN AMERICAN NAVAL OFFICER WHO BOMBED THE BARBARY PIRATES AT TRIPOLI, UPON LEARNING THAT ALL THE OFFICERS ASSIGNED HIM WERE UNDER 30, PROTESTED: "**THEY HAVE GIVEN ME NOTHING BUT A PACK OF BOYS!**"

GRADUATES of VASSAR ORIGINALLY RECEIVED ONLY CERTIFICATES OF "*THE FIRST DEGREE OF LIBERAL ARTS*" BECAUSE IT WAS CONSIDERED UNSEEMLY FOR A WOMAN TO BE CALLED A BACHELOR OF ARTS

THE **SAW FISH** THE BICHIR, A FRESHWATER FISH OF AFRICA, HAS ON ITS BACK A SERIES OF FINLETS THAT WHEN UPRIGHT LOOK LIKE *THE TEETH OF A SAW*

LHASA THE CAPITAL OF TIBET, ON SUMMER DAYS REGISTERS 90 DEGREES AT NOON-- *AND ZERO AT MIDNIGHT*

JAMES K. POLK THE FIRST DARK-HORSE PRESIDENTIAL CANDIDATE IN AMERICA'S HISTORY, AND PROBABLY THE MOST UNKNOWN CHIEF EXECUTIVE, STRETCHED THE COUNTRY'S BORDERS TO THE PACIFIC *AND ADDED 1,000,000 SQ. MILES OF TERRITORY*

THE **TREE FROG** WHICH HAS SUCKERS ON ITS TOES, CAN HANG UPSIDE DOWN FROM TREE LIMBS

SIAMESE CANTALOUPES
Submitted by Thomas D'Amico, Jr.,
Milwaukee, Wis.

LON CHANEY
STARRED IN " LONDON
AFTER MIDNIGHT," IN 1927
-- *THE FIRST VAMPIRE
FILM MADE IN
AMERICA*

A **MAPLE LEAF**
MEASURING 12"x 12"
found by Mrs. Franth Wetherholts,
Mattoon, Illinois

A **STATUE**
OF GEORGE WASHINGTON
WAS MOVED FROM THE EAST LAWN OF THE CAPITOL
IN WASHINGTON, D.C., IN 1908, BECAUSE THE PUBLIC
*WAS OFFENDED BY THE NUDITY DISPLAYED
BY ITS GRECIAN GOD ATTIRE*

A STARFISH
SHELL
WITH A WATCH
IN ITS CENTER IS
USED FOR PROPHECIES
in Mrewa, Mashonaland,
Africa,
BY A WITCH DOCTOR
WHO BELIEVES IN
KEEPING UP WITH THE TIMES

THE SERPENTINE A SNAKE-SHAPED MUSICAL INSTRUMENT WAS USED IN ORCHESTRAS IN COLONIAL AMERICA IN THE 18th CENTURY

SEPP AN ALSATIAN DOG OWNED BY FERDINAND HATZINGER OF MUNICH, GERMANY, COULD BALANCE ON HIS NOSE A COFFEE SERVICE FOR FOUR

ROBERT COATES (1772-1848) A BRITISH ACTOR, OFTEN REWROTE SHAKESPEARE'S PLAYS TO SUIT HIS OWN TALENTS

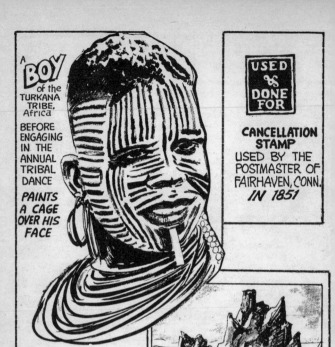

A **BOY** of the TURKANA TRIBE, Africa
BEFORE ENGAGING IN THE ANNUAL TRIBAL DANCE *PAINTS A CAGE OVER HIS FACE*

USED & DONE FOR

CANCELLATION STAMP USED BY THE POSTMASTER OF FAIRHAVEN, CONN. *IN 1851*

CHICK WITH **3** LEGS
Owned by Merlin and Marvin Greese, of Metairie, La.

THE CAVE-LIKE OPENINGS IN THE ROCKY CRAG OVERLOOKING THE GOREME VALLEY, ASIA MINOR, *ARE ACTUALLY CHURCHES CARVED IN THE STONE IN THE EARLY DAYS OF CHRISTIANITY*

THE ALLIGATOR GAR of the Southern United States *HAS NOT CHANGED IN 300,000,000 YEARS.*

THE ELABORATE FLORAL DESIGN WHICH DECORATES THE CITY HALL PLAZA IN OROTAVA IN THE CANARY ISLANDS FOR THE FESTIVAL OF CORPUS CHRISTI, IS CREATED SOLELY FROM *EARTH OF DIFFERENT COLORS*

A **BELL** in Uppsala, Sweden, HAS BEEN RUNG TWICE EACH DAY SINCE 1597 AS A MEMORIAL TO THE WOMAN WHO CAST IT --*THE WIFE OF KING JOHN III*

A **MAGNET** CAN PICK UP ONLY ONE ISSUE OF U.S. COIN -- *THE "WHITE" CENT OF 1943, WHICH CONTAINS IRON* Submitted by JACK REED Scottsdale, Arizona

THE **INDIAN HEAD** SO. GATEWAY ROCK, COLORADO SPRINGS, COLO. *NATURAL STONE FORMATION*

WOOD MARKED WITH *A PERFECT STAR*
Submitted by
CEISTA LITTLE,
Detroit, Mich.

KING **SAHALE SELASSIE**
of Shoa, Ethiopia,
CELEBRATED EACH NEW YEAR'S
*BY PERSONALLY PAYING
THE DEBTS OF EVERY PAUPER
IN HIS KINGDOM*

ELBURS, A TOWN ON THE SLOPE
of Mount Elburs, in Iran,
IS SO CONSTRUCTED THAT THE
ROOFS OF HOUSES ON ONE LEVEL
*SERVE AS THE STREET FOR THE
NEXT HIGHER ROW OF HOMES*

THE FERRY
CARRYING WORSHIPERS TO JAPAN'S MIYAJIMA SHRINE, HAS A PROW *RESEMBLING A FIERCE DRAGON*

DANIEL WEBSTER (1782-1852) WAS A BITTER FOE OF JOHN C. CALHOUN ON THE ISSUE OF SLAVERY, BUT WHEN CALHOUN DIED IN 1850, WEBSTER *DELIVERED THE EULOGY*

NAPOLEON'S HAT
IN THE FICHTEL MOUNTAINS
of Germany
A GIANT ROCKING STONE THAT LOOKS LIKE A COCKED HAT
-AND ALSO SHAKES SIDEWAYS AND NODS UP AND DOWN

Kitten
EATS
CORN ON
THE COB
Submitted by
THOMAS CARMICHAEL
Metairie, La.

A **RAILROAD**
in Stephansort, Papua,
IS POWERED BY OXEN

SIEVING THE BABY

AN ANCIENT TRADITION IN THE
DAKHLA OASIS OF THE LIBYAN
DESERT, *INVOLVES SHAKING EACH
7-DAY-OLD BABY IN A LARGE
SIEVE WITH A PINCH OF SALT AND
A LITTLE WHEAT, BARLEY AND RICE.*
THE GRAIN THAT FALLS TO THE
GROUND IS ALLOWED TO BLOW
AWAY IN THE BELIEF IT WILL
ASSURE A GOOD LIFE TO THE CHILD
WHEREVER HE MAY TRAVEL IN THE FUTURE

THE **ARCH OF TRIUMPH**
in Barcelona, Spain,
WAS ORIGINALLY
CONSTRUCTED AS
*THE ENTRANCE GATE TO THE
BARCELONA FAIR IN 1888*

168

THE FIRE FLOWER
(Epilobium Augustifolium)
ONLY GROWS ON SOIL
SEARED BY FIRE

JUDGE
JOHN G.
WILKIN

(1818-1889) of Middletown, N.Y.,
WHO PRACTICED LAW FOR 36 YEARS,
WAS SO SUSPICIOUS OF WOMEN THAT
HE NEVER REPRESENTED ONE IN COURT
*AND REFUSED TO PARTICIPATE
IN ANY TRANSACTION IN WHICH
A WOMAN WAS INVOLVED*

THE
TOMB
of Harispe
CHIEF of East Nigeria, Africa, IS
ADORNED BY A TABLEAU DEPICTING
THE CHIEF SEATED ON HIS THRONE
-AND UPHELD BY THE
*COMMANDER OF HIS ARMED FORCES
AND HIS PRIME MINISTER*

169

WINE DELIVERIES
TO ANCIENT BABYLON WERE
MADE VIA THE EUPHRATES RIVER
*IN ROUND BOATS THAT ALWAYS
CARRIED A DONKEY—*

AT BABYLON THE BOATS WERE
SOLD BECAUSE THEY COULD NOT
BE PROPELLED UPRIVER
AGAINST THE CURRENT— AND
THE TRIP HOME WAS MADE
ON THE DONKEY

PROLOGUE
CAMPOS
of Pará, Brazil,
HAD 3 BROTHERS NAMED
**CHAPTER,
ERRORS'**
and
EPILOGUE

THE **SANS SOUCI HOUSE**
in Siasconset, Mass.,
WAS ORIGINALLY PART OF A TWINE
FACTORY. ITS KITCHEN WAS A BOAT
HOUSE, AND ITS BRICKS WERE THE
BALLAST ON A WRECKED SHIP

WOOD CRATES
WERE USED AS BALLOT BOXES
IN NEBRASKA IN 1871, BUT
IN ONE ELECTION A CROOKED
OFFICIAL WAS SPOTTED
STUFFING FAKE BALLOTS
THROUGH A KNOTHOLE

OFFICIALS
IN THE DUTCH EAST INDIES
SHOWED THEIR RANK BY
*THE NUMBER OF RINGS
ON THE UMBRELLA THAT
SHIELDED THEM FROM
THE SUN*

**THE CHURCH OF SAN LORENZO
IN MIRANDA** , Rome,
WAS BUILT INSIDE THE COLUMNS OF
AN ANCIENT PAGAN TEMPLE ERECTED
BY EMPEROR ANTONINUS PIUS
1,800 YEARS AGO

THE **STATE CAPITOL**
OF OHIO, AT COLUMBUS, BECAUSE OF FINANCIAL AND LABOR TROUBLES AND A CHOLERA EPIDEMIC, WAS NOT COMPLETED *UNTIL 20 YEARS AFTER ITS CORNER-STONE WAS LAID*

CALF
OWNED BY DAN MARTIN OF BELLE PLAINE, IA., BORN ON THE **7**th DAY OF THE **7**th MONTH WITH A PERFECT **7** ON ITS FOREHEAD.

Submitted by Chester P. Fredericks Chicago, Ill.

JAN TARNOWSKI
POLISH STATESMAN, HAD **5** SONS *AND NAMED EVERY ONE OF THEM JAN*

172

TRIBESMEN OF Baluchistan, Pakistan, WEAR TROUSERS MADE FROM 40 YARDS OF CLOTH

"TIGER" A DOG OWNED BY CHRISTINE ALBERT, SHELLS AND EATS INDIAN NUTS Maspeth, N.Y.

THE WILLIAM PENN STATUE ATOP THE CITY HALL OF PHILADELPHIA, PA., 37 FEET HIGH AND WEIGHING 53,348 LBS., IS THE LARGEST SCULPTURE ON ANY BUILDING IN THE WORLD

173

THE TEMPLE OF TARISI
Tibet

IS ROOFED WITH SOLID-GOLD TILES VALUED TODAY AT $173,250!

THE CHURCH BUILT OF SNOW

William Kraut
of Enzweihingen, Germany,
AT THE AGE OF 8
**BUILT A 25-PEW
CHURCH OF SNOW**

THE BIRCH LEAF ROLLER

PROVIDES A CONTAINER FOR ITS EGGS AND FOOD FOR THE EMERGING LARVA BY MAKING EXACT INCISIONS IN A BIRCH LEAF *AND THEN ROLLING IT TO FORM AN INGENIOUS CONE*

AN ICE-CREAM MACHINE BOUGHT IN 1784 BY *GEORGE WASHINGTON*

THE *GROTTO* OF THE *ANNUNCIATION* in the Franciscan Monastery in Washington, D.C., IS SO FAITHFUL A COPY OF THE CHAPEL in Nazareth, Israel, *THAT IT HAS EVEN REPRODUCED EXACTLY A COLUMN FROM WHICH A PIECE WAS CUT OUT BY ROBBERS WHO INVADED THE ORIGINAL CHAPEL IN 1638 SEEKING HIDDEN TREASURE*

A *MARRIED WOMAN* of the Sudan WEARS HER GOLD WEDDING RING *IN HER NOSE*

A **SINGLE PARAMECIUM** ONLY 1/125TH OF AN INCH LONG *COULD IN 5 YEARS PRODUCE A MASS OF OFFSPRING FILLING AN AREA* **10,000 TIMES THE SIZE OF THE EARTH**

THE **STATUE** WITHOUT A FACE
Kyrene, Libya,
A STATUE ERECTED TO HONOR HIS WIFE, BY AN ANCIENT ROMAN *WHO FELT SHE WAS SO BEAUTIFUL, NO SCULPTURED FACE WOULD DO HER JUSTICE*

THE **TREES** IN FRONT OF
The Potala Palace of the
Dalai Lama of Tibet
HAVE BEEN SO TWISTED BY THE VIOLENT WINDS THEY *LOOK LIKE CORKSCREWS*

The **LANTERN FLY**
of Dutch Guiana
IS NOT A FLY AND CASTS NO LIGHT—

IT IS A BUG, AND THE "LANTERN" PROTRUDING FROM ITS HEAD IS ALWAYS DARK

HORSE CARTS in Mongolia ARE CONSTRUCTED *WITHOUT A SINGLE NAIL*

A **SCOLD'S BRIDLE** USED ON NAGGING WOMEN IN 17th-CENTURY GERMANY, WAS AN IRON MASK *WITH A BIT THAT HELD THE TONGUE STILL AND A BELL THAT RANG IF THE WEARER MOVED HER HEAD*

THE LOTTERY OF DEATH!
George Bibb Crittenden
1812 - 1880

ONE OF THE TEXANS FORCED BY THEIR MEXICAN CAPTORS TO DRAW LOTS TO DETERMINE WHICH WOULD DIE, SELECTED A LUCKY WHITE BEAN *-BUT GAVE IT TO A FELLOW PRISONER WHO HAD A WIFE AND CHILDREN*

HE DREW AGAIN FOR HIS OWN FATE *-AND AGAIN PICKED A WHITE BEAN*
1843

A GAME BOARD FOUND BY A HARVARD EXPEDITION IN IRELAND HAD BEEN CARVED OUT OF YEW WOOD *IN THE 10TH CENTURY*

WAI WAI TRIBESMEN
OF BRITISH GUIANA AND BRAZIL THRUST **2** SCARLET MACAW FEATHERS THROUGH THE SEPTUM OF THEIR NOSE --TO LOOK *LIKE HANDLEBAR MOUSTACHES*

A WINDMILL THAT ONCE STOOD IN THE CENTER OF LAS VEGAS, N.M., WAS TORN DOWN IN 1880 IN THE BELIEF THE WATER IN ITS WELL HAD BEEN CONTAMINATED BECAUSE *SO MANY MEN HAD BEEN HUNG FROM IT*

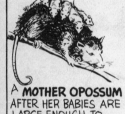

A **MOTHER OPOSSUM** AFTER HER BABIES ARE LARGE ENOUGH TO LEAVE HER POUCH, *CARRIES THEM AROUND ON HER BACK*

WHEN MEN WERE MEN
MEN IN AMERICA IN THE 1700's, HAVING SHAVED THEIR HEADS TO ACCOMMODATE THE PERIOD'S HOT WIGS, USUALLY WORE TURBANS INDOORS AND *SLEPT IN NEGLIGEE CAPS*

THE FIRST HOMES
BUILT BY THE PILGRIMS AND PURITANS IN AMERICA *WERE WIGWAMS MADE OF BARK, THATCH AND WATTLES DAUBED WITH MUD*

179

A WIDE TURBAN
IS DONNED BY WOMEN OF SZECHWAN, CHINA,
IN THE BELIEF IT WILL **CURE A HEADACHE**

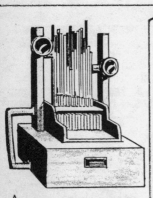

A **ROMAN PIPE ORGAN**
IN THE AQUINCUM MUSEUM
IN BUDAPEST, HUNGARY,
IS PLAYABLE AFTER
2,000 YEARS

ROLLER SKATES
ADVERTISED
IN LONDON,
ENGLAND,
IN THE 1800's,
WERE
ACTUALLY
SMALL
TRICYCLES

THE LUCKIEST GIRLS IN THE WORLD!
A GIRL of the LENGUA TRIBE of Bolivia CAN CHOOSE AS HER HUSBAND ANY BACHELOR IN THE TRIBE -AND *HE CAN'T SAY NO!*

THE TOWN HALL
OF NORTH SALEM, N.Y., BUILT IN 1773 AS A MANOR HOUSE, *HAS ALSO SERVED AS AN ACADEMY, COURTHOUSE AND JAIL*

THE **KAPELL BRIDGE** at Lucerne, Switzerland, WAS CONSTRUCTED **643** YEARS AGO

THE MANOR OF BENTLEY STILL STANDING ON STATEN ISLAND, N.Y., WAS THE SITE OF *THE FIRST PEACE CONFERENCE IN AMERICA* LORD HOWE, COMMANDER OF THE BRITISH FORCES, MET BENJAMIN FRANKLIN, JOHN ADAMS AND EDWARD RUTLEDGE HERE IN 1776

ADDISON PITT AN ACTOR FROM LONDON, ENGLAND, SPOKE THE LAST LINES UTTERED ON THE STAGE OF FAMOUS OLD MACAULEY'S THEATER IN LOUISVILLE, KY.

HALF A CENTURY EARLIER, THE FIRST LINES SPOKEN IN THAT THEATER WERE *DELIVERED BY PITT'S ACTRESS MOTHER, FANNY ADDISON*

A WALKING-STICK CAMERA INVENTED BY A. LEHMANN of Berlin, Germany, IN 1903

THE **AYE-AYE** FOUND ONLY IN MADAGASCAR, IS EQUIPPED WITH A LONG MIDDLE FINGER THAT ENABLES IT TO DIG GRUBS OUT OF TREES

ROY ACUFF THE TENNESSEAN CALLED THE FATHER OF COUNTRY MUSIC, HAD PLANNED TO BE A PROFESSIONAL BASEBALL PLAYER--*BUT HIS BALL CAREER ENDED ABRUPTLY DURING SUMMER TRAINING WITH THE YANKEES WHEN HE SUFFERED A SUNSTROKE*

THE **CATHEDRAL** of **NOTRE DAME** IN REIMS, FRANCE, WAS STARTED IN 1211 AND COMPLETED IN 1430 --*219 YEARS LATER*

183

TANKARDS AND **TABLEWARE** USED BY THE COLONISTS AT PLYMOUTH WERE ALMOST ENTIRELY **WOODEN**

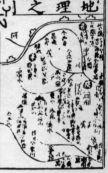

THE OLDEST PRINTED MAP A MAP OF WESTERN CHINA SHOWING PART OF THE GREAT WALL --*PRINTED IN 1155*

ANTOINE de la Mothe **CADILLAC** (1656-1730) THE FRENCH SOLDIER WHO FOUNDED DETROIT, MICH, WHO WAS COURAGEOUS AND WITTY, BUT HAD A VERY LONG NOSE, *INSPIRED EDMOND ROSTAND'S "CYRANO de BERGERAC"*

RINSING BOWLS WERE A SOCIAL NECESSITY IN COLONIAL AMERICA SINCE MANY WINES WERE SERVED *AND THE GLASSES HAD TO BE RINSED BETWEEN EACH CHANGE OF WINE*

THE **KAGU BIRD** OF NEW CALEDONIA, WHICH IS FLIGHTLESS, HAS A VOICE THAT SOUNDS LIKE A PUPPY DOG

MRS. ENOS BROWN OF TRAVER HOLLOW, N.Y., WAS FAMED IN THE LATE 19th CENTURY AS A **BEAR HUNTER**

A **TRAVELING TRUNK** OFFERED FOR SALE IN WOLVERHAMPTON, ENGLAND, IN THE 1800's, CONVERTED INTO A *BATHTUB*

HUGE LAND CRABS in CUBA, *CAN OUTRACE A HORSE*

The **IBIS** IS CONSIDERED SO SACRED BY THE OSIRIS CULT OF EGYPT THAT A SPECIAL CEMETERY HALF A MILE SQUARE WAS ESTABLISHED AT ABYDOS, EGYPT, FOR MUMMIES OF THESE WINGED COURIERS OF THE GODS

EUGLENA VIRIDIS A MINUTE WATER ORGANISM CALLED THE PUPIL OF THE EYE *CONSTANTLY CHANGES ITS SHAPE*

THE **ZEBRA FISH** OF THE INDIAN OCEAN HAS ZEBRA-LIKE STRIPES

THE **BOERS** RECRUITED AT THE START OF THE BOER WAR AGAINST THE BRITISH IN 1899, WERE *SUBJECT TO SERVICE FROM 16 TO 65, WORE THEIR OWN CLOTHING, CARRIED THEIR OWN RIFLES, AND WERE NOT PAID*

THE **OLDEST BRICK PAGODA** IN CHINA

THE BUDDHIST TEMPLE OF SUNG-YUEH SSU AT SUNG SHAN, HONAN, WHICH HAS 12 SIDES AND 15 STORIES, WAS BUILT OF BRICK **453 YEARS AGO**

GEORGE TAYLOR
OF EASTON, PA.,
ONE OF THE SIGNERS OF THE
DECLARATION OF INDEPENDENCE,
*CAME TO AMERICA AS
AN INDENTURED SERVANT*

A **WATCH CAMERA**
PATENTED BY
M. NIELL IN 1903,
TOOK PICTURES
THROUGH ITS STEM

A **LIGHTHOUSE** BUILT BY THE ROMANS AT BOULOGNE ON THE NORTH COAST OF FRANCE, SERVED AS A WARNING TO SHIPS AT SEA *FOR 1,400 YEARS*

MRS. **EDITH BOLLING GALT WILSON**
THE WIFE OF PRES. WOODROW WILSON, VIRTUALLY RAN THE COUNTRY DURING HER HUSBAND'S LONG ILLNESS -- *YET SHE OPPOSED FEMALE SUFFRAGE*

POST CARD
MAILED FROM
Princeton, N.J.,
AND DELIVERED
TO CHARLES A.
KEARNS OF
Wayne, N.J.

ALTHOUGH IT CARRIED NO NAME OR ADDRESS

The **NAME** of the **LAST KING OF KAFFA** Africa

WAS KNOWN TO ONLY **7 PEOPLE**—

THE SEVEN DIGNITARIES GAVE THE MONARCH THE NAME GAKI SHEROTSKO —AND KEPT IT SECRET IN THE BELIEF THE KING COULD NOT BE HARMED BY ANYONE WHO DIDN'T KNOW HIS NAME

THORSTEIN VEBLEN (1857-1929) POLITICAL ECONOMIST, SOCIOLOGIST AND SOCIAL CRITIC, WHO WAS BORN AND REARED IN A NORWEGIAN COMMUNITY IN WISCONSIN, *SPOKE NO ENGLISH UNTIL HE WENT TO COLLEGE*

THE BEACHES
of Patagonia, in So. America,
ARE COVERED AFTER
HIGH TIDE WITH
*MILLIONS OF SARDINES
AND OTHER FISH*

THE 10th EARL of COVENTRY
(1838 - 1930)
HELD HIS TITLE FOR
86 YEARS

THE CHURCH OF LE PLANÈS
in France
ORIGINALLY WAS CONSTRUCTED
AS THE TOMB OF AN ARAB
REBEL NAMED MUNAZA WHO
WAS EXECUTED DURING A
MOORISH INVASION
OF FRANCE IN 721

MAJOR JOHN DYKE ACLAND
A BRITISH MILITARY OFFICER,
WHO FOUGHT AGAINST THE
COLONIES IN THE AMERICAN
REVOLUTION, WAS SEVERELY
WOUNDED AND MADE A PRISONER
-- YET UPON HIS RETURN
TO ENGLAND HE FOUGHT
A DUEL WITH ANOTHER
BRITISH OFFICER WHO HAD
MALIGNED THE AMERICANS

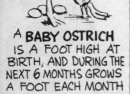

A **BABY OSTRICH**
IS A FOOT HIGH AT
BIRTH, AND DURING THE
NEXT 6 MONTHS GROWS
A FOOT EACH MONTH

**ONE OF THE
LANTERNS** PLACED IN
BOSTON'S OLD
NORTH CHURCH
IN 1775, AS A
SIGNAL TO PAUL
REVERE, IS
STILL IN WORK-
ABLE CONDITION

THE WANTON-LYMAN-HAZARD HOUSE BUILT IN NEWPORT, R.I., IN 1675, IS THE *OLDEST HOUSE IN NEWPORT*

Sir HARRY LAUDER (1870-1950) WHO BECAME WORLD FAMOUS FOR HIS SONGS IN SCOTTISH DIALECT, LAUNCHED HIS PROFESSIONAL CAREER *SINGING AN IRISH SONG*

MARBLEHEAD LIGHTHOUSE BUILT ON MARBLEHEAD PENINSULA IN 1821, *IS THE OLDEST LIGHTHOUSE IN OHIO*